To A[...]

Here's [...]

newfound love of

CYCLING IN
THE
SOUTH BAY

two wheeling and

mandex. I hope our

paths cross more on

the road or in a

Seth Davidson

bar!

[signature]

12/31/2013

For Barbara

CONTENTS

CYCLING IN THE SOUTH BAY

ACKNOWLEDGMENTS

Thank you, Barbara Radnofsky. Of all the people in this world, I admire you most.

Thank you, Chris Gregory, for your encouragement and inspiration.

Thank you, Derek Brauch, for the criticism and the beer.

Thank you, Lesli Cohen, for the razor sharp editing and the lessons on "hearken" and "scot-free."

Thank you, Danny Munson, for the lens.

Thank you, Michael Marckx. I can see clearly now.

Thank you, Jack Daugherty and Yukon Cornelius, the two funniest people I know.

Thank you, Michael Norris, for your humanity.

Thank you, Fields. You will always be the greatest.

Thank you, Roger Worthington, for helping me even when you tried your hardest not to.

Thank you, Phil Tomlin, Jack Pritchard, and Jay Aust, for dealing the bicycle crack.

Thank you, Fletcher. Arf.

Thank you, racers and chasers, hammerheads and wankers. You are the South Bay.

Thank you, Yasuko. I love you most of all.

SETH DAVIDSON

FOREWORD

Read this book. It's all true except for the parts that Seth made up, which appears to be all of it. If you're a cyclist, you'll laugh because you probably have the same collection of characters in your group. If you're not a cyclist, read this book and rejoice that this is not your passion!

Greg Leibert
August, 2013
Leadville, Colorado

SETH DAVIDSON

LANCE'S SMELLY JOCKSTRAP AND ME

It started innocently enough. I had joined Twitter a few months back. Then a couple of evenings later I looked at Twitter's "recommendations" about whom I should follow. One of the recommendations was Lance.

I clicked on him to browse a few of his tweets. From the first tweet they came flooding back, memories as sharp and clear as if it all happened yesterday. As I scrolled down through the tens, then the hundreds of tweets, I was astounded at how Lance had changed.

I'd long known that he had changed from the time we first met in January of 1991 simply because I had followed the extraordinary course of his life and career. But his ticker tape parade of thoughts and remarks and comments on Twitter brought into stark relief the difference between this world-famous celebrity and the teenager who once tried to sell me the parts off his bike.

His choice of words, his facility with them on Twitter, and his understanding that his words shaped the thoughts of others all pointed to the unmistakable fact that he is a very intelligent man. If you had told me in 1991 that he was a toweringly bright guy, when the only thing he wanted to know about the girl at the copy shop who I'd had print and bind his resume was whether or not she had big boobs, I would have laughed.

I'm not laughing now.

These memories seared home the fact that he used to be a real person. Before he became a juggernaut, then a superstar, then a metaphor, and now, a post-modern retired celebrity athlete, disgraced drug cheat, seven-time TdF strippee, and the defendant in numerous state and federal lawsuits, before all that he was a just a young man with a compelling story and a once-in-a-generation set of genes. I want to share those memories with you on the off chance that a few of them might actually have happened. I want to share them because whatever you think of Lance, and whatever you've read about him, you haven't read this.

May I?

My intersection with Lance was natural enough. I'm a jock sniffer. Put me around a great athlete, and something warm and fuzzy comes over me. My nose starts tickling, then twitching, and pretty soon I'm nuzzling around in his jockey strap, snurfling at the sweat, the curly hairs, and the residue of whatever else might be left down in that musty cotton bag.

I can say this with no trace of shame because the chances are excellent that you're a jock sniffer, too. Go to any bike race and you'll see a small cluster around the Stud. Watch what happens at major sporting events when ol' Sweatnglory shows up to receive his plaque, or when the Anointed One wins the big game. The bigger the star, the more recklessly people will fight to plunge their noses as deeply as they can into the dank boulder holder. Sniffers can't help jock sniffing in the presence of successful athletes because it hearkens to our primitive history. It's in our genes to genuflect before the hairy one who slew the enemy and paraded around with his head on a pike.

The athletes themselves appear to hold jock sniffers in contempt, and in fact they do. But they also love them, kind of like the man feels about the "woman" in a men's prison. Without jock sniffers, the greatest athlete in the world would be just another pair of nuts.

When I first caught the faintest whiff of Lance's jock

I had returned to Austin from an internship with a German law firm in Tokyo in order to pick up law school where I'd dumped it, unceremoniously, a year and a half before. One of the first calls I made was to Fields, who was running Eurosport over on 32nd Street, where the old Bice Cyclery used to be.

"You back?" he asked.

"Yeah."

"I got a VHS of the world championships in Utsunomiya. That was some course."

"It was awesome. I got to see Delgado, Indurain, Kelly, LeMond, and got to ride in the Spanish team's car when I took them on a training ride up through Nikko, Kirifuri-kogen, and some other cool places."

"Did you watch the amateur race?"

"Not really."

"One of the guys who was in that race lives here. Armstrong. Lance Armstrong. He would have won the race if he hadn't attacked every single lap."

"Oh." I was embarrassed to say that I'd paid no attention to the U.S. amateur team, not at the huge welcoming party with two barbecued cows and a massive fireworks display thrown by the city for the racers down on the Kinugawa River, not at the reception at the Utsunomiya Grand Hotel, not even at the race itself. I couldn't have picked Lance out of a crowd of two.

"He's coming down to the shop tomorrow morning to ride. You been riding?"

"Yeah, somewhat."

"Well, you should come join us. It will be the hardest ride of your life."

The path of truth

Whatever Fields was, he was factual, as in "Midwestern factual." And when it came to "hard" he was something of a connoisseur. When I first got the strange idea that I wanted to race bikes, he introduced me to motor pacing. Dogbait and he shared a 50cc Honda scooter that they had borrowed from Buffalo Russ. We'd pedal out of town to the intersection of FM 969 and FM 973, Dogbait would ramp up the scooter, and one of us would sit behind the motor all the way to Webberville, nine very unpleasant miles. In Webberville we'd switch places. Never once did I make it all the way back to FM 973, usually coming off the motor in the last mile.

We came to call that road the Path of Truth because there was no hiding. You either held the motor or you didn't. Even today when I think about the pain, misery, suffering, and defeat from those sessions, I get tingles up and down my legs. They say your body and mind have the ability to remember pleasure but to forget pain. "They" have never done the Path of Truth in a cold February crosswind at thirty mph trying to find a nonexistent draft behind a tiny scooter.

"Is it going to be harder than the Path of Truth?"

Fields didn't hesitate. "Yes."

That night I tossed and turned. A beatdown was on its way, that was certain. But how bad a beatdown? Would I finish the ride? Who was Lance Armstrong?

The next morning I rolled down to the shop from my married students' apartment on Lake Austin Boulevard. I arrived a few minutes early. Lance got there exactly on time. "So you were in Utsunomiya?" he asked.

"Yes."

"Hard race."

I didn't know what to say, as I'd been sipping coffee and eating snacks in the VIP section at the start/finish. "It sure looked like it."

A fourth person started with us, but I don't remember his name. What I do remember is hitting the bottom of the climb on Lime Creek Road and already feeling like I'd been in the saddle for five hours. Simply sitting on Lance's wheel took every bit of strength and concentration I could muster. He breezily chatted all the way up the climb as our #4 companion dropped away permanently, and Fields and I struggled to keep the pace. For Lance it was effortless, and he was obviously going slowly so that we could stay together.

On the top we turned right on FM 1431. "Wanna buy these Dura-Ace STI shifters and gruppo?" he asked. "I'm leaving Subaru after I turn pro. I'll make you a deal."

"Who are you going to be riding with?"

"I don't know. I've got a contract from Motorola. You're a lawyer, right? Maybe you could look it over for me?"

"I'm not a lawyer, I'm a law student. I can't really give you any legal advice."

"Aw, sure you can. Come over to my place after the ride and look at the contract. You'll know more about it than I do. Maybe you can tell me if I'm getting a good deal." He was an optimist, thinking I'd still be alive after the ride.

Somehow I finished it, a mere sixty mile leg stretcher that remains the fastest I've ever gone that distance on a bike. I was destroyed, Fields was wrecked, and Lance hadn't yet ridden his bike that day. After he deposited us at the shop, two smoking piles of goo, Lance went out for a real ride. I still can't imagine what one of those is.

The blind leading the partially blind

That afternoon I went over to his apartment on Shoal Creek, just down from the tennis courts at the intersection of 24th and Lamar. I was struck by how orderly and put together his place was. For a nineteen-year-old kid, he sure seemed to have clear ideas of how he wanted the world around him to be. It wouldn't be until I reached my late forties that I ever lived in an apartment half as neat as his.

"Here's the contract."

I tried to protest again, but he wasn't interested. I was as close to a lawyer as anyone he knew, and he liked and trusted me. Perhaps "trusted" isn't the right word, but I read the thing and tried to understand it. As we talked it over I asked, "Can you show me a copy of your race resume?"

"Yeah, sure." He dug out a three-page typewritten list of results. It was an extraordinary rendition of firsts and seconds in ten-point type that went on and on and on.

"Wow, dude," I said. "Where are your press clippings?"

"My what?"

"Press clippings. Surely you've been written up in the local newspapers."

He laughed. "My mom keeps that stuff. It's in Plano."

"You might be able to negotiate better terms, or maybe you could get a better offer from a European team. But you'll need a first-rate bio and nicely bound folder to put your press clippings in." I was thinking a five or six-page document including his press mentions that summed up who he was, what he'd done, and where he was going.

"I could get you the stuff. I'll drive back home tomorrow and could have it here the day after. Is that something you can do? I'll pay you."

"You don't have to pay me. Just get me the stuff and I'll put something together. These results are astounding. People ought to be falling all over themselves to get you on their team. Wow."

Two days later Lance called. "Hey, man, I'm back. I got the stuff. You want to come over and get it?"

"Sure." I drove to his place. He was standing outside, next to his car. I think he had some kind of pale blue Dodge.

"Stuff's in the trunk." He opened it. I stared, then I stared again.

"Dude. What is that?" The cavernous trunk of the Dodge was filled with a stack of newspapers and magazines as long as my arm.

"Those are my press clippings."

"All that is about you?"

He looked at me, not modestly, not arrogantly, just matter-of-factly. He looked at me the way you'd look at someone if you were making them conform to your vision of how the world was going to be. "Yes."

Big boobs and a whole lotta Rosie

I brought the stack home and embarked on a weeklong project. Every couple of days Lance would call. He was never overtly excited, but it hadn't escaped my attention that the minute he had seen the value of putting together his press clippings, he'd jumped in the car and driven four hours to Plano and back. Now that I was working on it, he wanted to know how it was going. He was keeping tabs on the story of his brief athletic life, and he was keeping tabs on the person in charge of it. He was nineteen years old and keeping tabs, managing the project. How about that?

This made a strange impression on me. I was eight years older. I'd graduated from college. I was enrolled in one of the nation's top law schools. I was doing this as a favor to a punk bike racer, but Lance the punk was in charge. He wasn't in charge rudely, or roughly, or insultingly, but he was unmistakably in charge.

I wound up with the makings for an 8-1/2" x 11" booklet that would easily be a hundred pages long. It included magazine covers, encomiums by sports writers, and terse tales of the swath of destruction he'd left in his wake in almost every event he'd ever entered. I started to get a sense of the force of nature I'd bumped up against. This wasn't just any old jockstrap. This might be, I thought, the biggest, gnarliest, sweatiest jockstrap of all time. "For Dog's sake," I kept telling myself. "He's only nineteen."

There was a little copy shop just off the corner of Red River and Medical Arts near the law school. I took in the manuscript of clippings and photos and struck up a conversation with the girl running the shop, whose name was Rosie. "This," I told her, "is the short history of a guy who's going to be the greatest cyclist this country has ever known."

Rosie lit up. "Really?" My description must have sounded so dramatic and exciting. She leafed through the pages. "Wow. This is incredible. He's so good looking." Then she batted her eyes at me. "Can I meet him?"

I laughed. "I'll see what I can do."

The next day I picked up the bound final copy. I'd included an introduction, and had spent a long time trying to get it right. Of course, I had gotten it wrong. While leafing through the pages trying to organize it, and getting intoxicated by the scruffy smell of that sweaty old jockstrap, I'd let my creativity run wild. "Lance Armstrong," I wrote, "is destined to become the greatest cyclist since Eddy Merckx."

Now I looked at the finished product. "What a pile of crap," I thought. "This kid's no Eddy Merckx."

If it bothered Lance, he didn't show it. I had made five copies, and gave them to him. He leafed through the finished product carefully. "Thanks." I could tell he liked it. Then he reached into his wallet and proffered $200. "Here. I said I'd pay you."

I laughed. "I don't want your money. Glad to help."

He smiled back, politely, but his outstretched hand didn't budge. "I said I'd pay you."

I felt it again, keenly. He was in charge. He did what he said he was going to do, and the world was going to look the way he wanted it to look. I took the money. "The gal at the copy shop was mightily impressed. Said she'd love to meet you."

His eyes lit up and suddenly he was a nineteen year-old kid thinking about a hookup. "Big tits? I like bit tits. What's her name?"

"Rosie. Tits, not so big."

"I'll pass," he said firmly, with no hesitation and no more curiosity. The kid was in charge even when it came to his dick.

What's in it for me?

Lance became a distraction to my studies. I couldn't stop thinking about him. More to the point, I couldn't stop doing what everyone else who knew him had been doing, and what the rest of the world would soon be doing, too: Trying to figure out how to make a buck off this prodigy. What I was too stupid to realize was that Lance had long ago understood that others wanted what he had, and that the name of the game was, and would always be, keeping the upper hand from the cheats and the liars and the con men and the sniffers, especially the sniffers.

As I struggled with the nascent idea of how to turn him into my own private cash cow, but had no clear idea about how to do it, he had already developed an effective strategy for handling the jock sniffing, wannabe leeches like me who surround every person with great athletic talent. Give them a whiff, stay in control, and play them first before they play you; it's no different from winning a mass start bike race. This is the quality that would separate Lance from the basketball and football players who were multimillionaires one day and paupers the next.

At the time there was a new publication, long since defunct, called Texas Cyclist, or maybe it was Texas Bicyclist. I hit upon an idea. I'd pitch an article to them about Lance. I called the editor and they immediately agreed. I called Lance and he was game. The next day I was back at his apartment.

We talked for about an hour. Some of the things he said I remember with crystal clarity: "When I watch the Tour on TV, I visualize myself winning it," or "I'm a bigger rider, more like a Merckx or an Indurain, so those are the guys I try to emulate." There I sat, listening to a guy talk with a straight face about visualizing a Tour victory and comparing himself to Eddy and Big Mig. I took a few notes and basked in what was now the full-fledged odor of his steaming strap.

I got home and was giddy, so I wrote a long, fawning article and threw in a bunch of things he never said, all designed to make him look great and to inject myself into the awesome reality of Lance. I was the fanboy of all fanboys, a grown man with a family and the beginnings of a legitimate career, and there I sat, licking the spittle and sniffing the jock of a teenage athlete.

It was not my finest hour, but the final piece was tremendous. The magazine loved it. Lance liked it too, but he saw through the bullshit and the fabricated quotes in an instant. He never said anything about it or criticized me for it, but it proved what he'd suggested all along but never had to say. He was the better person, and he was in charge.

What's with the pink?

The next time I talked to Fields he said, "Are you going to the Tuesday Nighter out at Nuckols Crossing? Lance is gonna ride out there with us and do the race."

"Sure," I said.

My helmet was styrofoam with a fabric cover.

The fabric cover was gaudy pink. Lance looked at it and laughed. "What's with the pink?" For some reason, I'm not sure why, it stung. There's nothing worse than having your favorite jockstrap make fun of your pink helmet cover.

We got to the course and the race started. For the first lap we sat in the back and chatted. We came through the start/finish and crested the hill. Off in the distance were two tiny specks. "Are those guys off the front?" he asked.

"Yeah," I said. "They're gone. So much for this race."

He looked at me funny. Without getting out of the saddle, he pushed the pedals harder. In a few seconds he had rocketed off the front, never getting out of the saddle or even appearing to exert himself. I watched him vanish up the road. He caught the breakaway, dropped it, and won the race so far head of the next finisher that it was as if he had been in an entirely different race which, come to think of it, he was.

That was the last time we rode together. I may have spoken with him a time or two before I finished law school in May and moved to Japan, but I don't remember it if I did.

Nuts! Or, the world's most famous lateral orchiectomy

A couple of years after settling down in the upstairs bedroom of my in-law's home and beginning what would become an illustrious career as a world-famous English teacher in Japan ("What did you do today?" "Do you like music?" "I'm from Texas.") I heard the big news. Lance had won the professional world road race championships in Oslo. I called his mom in Plano and congratulated her. She told me with excitement and pride about how she got to meet the King of Norway. Sometime later I read about his death sentence when he'd been diagnosed with cancer, and called Linda again. We spoke briefly, and I told her how much I hoped Lance would pull through. She handed the phone over to her husband, a rather gruff guy. "He's gonna be just fine. He's gonna be A-okay."

"No," I thought. "He's going to be dead." It was a funny feeling, that kid who'd held all the cards and played them so well, never laying down anything but aces, the kid who, before he was twenty already knew how the world was going to look, dead from cancer before he even reached thirty.

We all know how that story ended. He pulled seven aces out of his ass and won the biggest bike race in the world seven times in a row. And then it all unraveled in a soap opera, with Oprah presiding over his demise. Even at the very end when no one believed him anymore he came across as still in charge, still playing the jock sniffers before they played him, still shitting aces.

He was a lot more complicated in 2013 than he was in 1991, but that residual admiration, that lingering aroma of the jock, that primal bowing of the head before the chieftain, there's something there that won't ever go away, at least for me. I've sat on the wheel, suffered a beatdown by one of the greatest riders ever, and finished the ride. Forget that he never broke a sweat.

If you've ever read *Jitterbug Perfume* by Tom Robbins, you'll get why smell overpowers the rational brain and makes us, once again, reptiles. As far as my Lance predictions go, I have a lifetime batting average of .500: Greatest cyclist since Eddy Merckx, check. Dead from cancer, not so much.

One night I was at Cynergy Cycles in Santa Monica, and who should walk in to buy a tire but the Garmin pro racer Tom Danielson. He hung around for a few minutes and chatted with us old farts. He was personable, engaging, and happy to talk, and after we prodded him he told us a few tales about some of the climbing records he has set in his career. His tale about breaking Lance's record on the Madone outside of Nice by forty seconds had us hanging on every word.

And I couldn't help thinking as my nose perked up, "What's that smell?"

CAPTAIN OVERPANTS

Mrs. Wankmeister and I were coming home along Palos Verdes Drive North one day when we approached a cycling dude from the rear. He had a very fine Cannondale, a very fine Shimano electronic transmission, a very fine Specialized helmet, very fine Sidi shoes, and a very fine commemorative jersey from the century ride he'd completed with 10,000 of his closest friends. It was purple and green and yellow and brown and white and black and red and olive. It was styling.

"What a wanker!" I said.

"Why he's wanker?"

"Look at those shorts. Dude is wearing loose khaki riding pants."

"Oh. Why that's a bad?"

"Those are called 'dickhiders' and signify pure wanker."

"What's dickhiding?"

"Not hiding. Hider. Dude's riding ten grand in bike and assorted paraphernalia but he's afraid to wear lycra because he's embarrassed to show his package."

"His chin-chin?"

"Yep." Mrs. WM and I often speak Japlish together.

"Why he's ashamed of tiny chin-chin? Asian girl's gonna wear little tight thing shows tiny oppai. Why he's not gonna show tiny chin-chin? Smart shopper wanna see it before she buy it."

"I dunno. But any time you see some dude wearing floppy shorts on a racing bike, it's because he doesn't want you postal inspector chicks to examine his package."

"He don't oughta be ashamed about no tiny chin-chin. I don't wanna see no big chin-chin in a bike shorts. Makes me sick, looking nasty all sticking out like bones and bagels."

"Dudes I ride with, you don't have to worry about that."

"Onna bike I don't wanna see no big nasty chin-chin poking in the lycra shorty pants with a pokey tip. Tiny chin-chin fits in the pants nice and don't make a lump. Like a girl's jeans. That's why a boy's jeans look nasty and not smooth. Gotta big lumpy donut and pokey in the middle not girl's smooth line."

"I'll try to remember that the next time I go shopping for jeans."

"But offa bike without no shorts it's okay if a big chin-chin. But not too big like a German sausage. Kind of middle size is best. Offa bike tiny chin-chin it's a kind of like a bumblebee who's not got the stinger. It's the disappointment."

We pulled up to the dude at the light. Mrs. Wankmeister rolled down the window. "Don't you worry about your chin-chin!" she said with a smile.

"My what?"

"Your chin-chin. It's a okay one nobody looking it just don't poke out like bones and bagels."

The dude looked seriously perplexed. Then we drove off.

FIELDS

My adventures in the South Bay of Los Angeles actually began a long time ago in a galaxy far, far away. In March 1985, Johnny Weltz and some of his Danish national teammates had come to Austin to race the Tour of Texas. Most of the foreign teams stayed at the Villa Capri, a cheap motel nestled cozily in the shadow of the elevated lanes of I-35, and in the morning they would do various training rides as they readied for the stage race which started the following week.

The Villa Capri, like so many other awful things about Old Austin, got torn down so that we could think fondly about it now that it's no longer there. I wish someone would do that to the Erwin Center.

It was incredible to see the cream of the amateur peloton right there in Austin, before it was ATX, before it was SXSW, before it was anything other than a college town with lots of hippies and the state legislature, back when it was "thirty square miles surrounded by reality" and the only airplanes that flew into Bergstrom were military. I'd been desperate to go on a training ride with one of the Euro groups, and

Fields, sick of the whining, said "Just do it. Show up. Roll out when they roll out. What are they going to do, fire you? It's not 'Breaking Away,' you knucklehead."

Does anyone here speak English?

I picked a group that turned out to be the Norwegian national team. They were riding with some of the Danes, and Johnny Weltz was one of them. The group was ten riders strong, and they all spoke perfect English. "Where are you riding to?" I asked.

"We want to do some miles so we are going out to the town called Burnet on the road called 183 and coming back on the road called 1431."

"Do you mind if I come along?"

The Norseman looked at my poorly developed legs. "It will be a long ride."

U.S. 183 had a wide shoulder and hardly any traffic back then, especially once you left town. The team car followed us. I was the only local freddie who had crashed the ride, and my addition resulted in an uneven number of riders, so I was paired with someone different every few minutes. In the rotation, everyone took paired five-minute pulls and then swung off. After a couple of hours I started to get hungry, and this was long before Clif or GU or Stinger or anything remotely like it. This was the era of banana or PB sandwich if you had the sense to pack it, or, most commonly, the era of "Pray for a convenience store."

It hadn't occurred to me that these guys would ride for three and a half hours without stopping. In a three-hour ride, The Violet Crown gang I normally rode with would have pulled over by then for the fifth time by a low-water crossing on a dirt road in order to smoke their tenth joint of the ride. The Euro dudes weren't stopping or smoking or doing anything except pedaling, and pedaling fast.

I started praying. As usual, my pleas went unheeded and my bonk began for real. I started to drift off the back, resigned to quitting before we'd even hit the halfway mark. Damn and triple damn.

A little encouragement goes a long way

The team car drove up. "Hey," the driver said. "You been riding strong. You are hunger knocking, eh?"

"Yeah," I said.

"I have a lot of food in the car."

My face said everything in reply.

"But I can't give you any. It is for the team." He kept staring at me as my spirit went from breaking to broken. "But still you should not give up. We are two miles from the Burnet. There is a store there with the water and the food. You can make it."

I forced myself back up to the peloton and somehow made it to the Burnet, where we pulled into the convenience store.

The driver got out. "You did okay. That was

hard for you."

Nobody rides for free

Once inside the store I realized I had no money. Of course I didn't. No one goes on a 125-mile beatdown with the Norwegian national team carrying money. Pride wouldn't let me ask for any and neither would pragmatism. If they wouldn't share their food they sure as hell weren't going to share their money. They were all talking in Norse anyway, and looking at me and grinning. I knew what they were saying.

"He wanted to ride with the team. He don't look like wants to ride so much now."

"Let's see how long it takes him to beg. I bet you ten kroner he will beg in two minutes."

"You think he's broke? I think he's broke. Look, he don't have any money! Har!"

By now the bonk was profound. I went to the back of the store and looked around. There was the coffee pot, but I didn't drink coffee and didn't have any money for it anyway. Next to the coffee pot, though, was a giant glass sugar dispenser. It clearly was meant for the coffee, but it didn't have a price tag on it.

I took the sugar dispenser and filled up my water bottle with most of the sugar. Then I went into the bathroom, turned on the tap and added hot water to dissolve the massive amount of sugar. I took a sip. It was the taste of life. I drained half the bottle, went back out and filled the bottle up again with more sugar. Suddenly, RR 1431 with its endless hills and winding tarmac wasn't looking so daunting.

Crime doesn't pay

As I headed for the door, the large gentleman covered in tattoos behind the counter yelled at me. This was before people got tattooed for fashion, and instead got tattooed as a way of saying "I've been in prison."

"Hey! Where do you think you're going?"

The Norsemen and Danes stopped and looked. The color drained from my face as my mind raced, trying to think of what to say. I'd been caught in the act. "Yeah, I'm talking to you," Mr. Tattoo said. "Think you can come into my store and steal all my sugar and walk the fuck off? This ain't fucking Russia or wherever the fuck you're from."

It was the "Russia" part that saved me.

"Excuse to me?" I said in my strongest fake Euro accent.

"I said you can't fucking take my sugar. Pony up, pal!" His red face had darkened redder.

"So sorry me, not good English. How problem?"

The Norwegians were doing all they could to keep from cracking up. Johnny Weltz came over and said in his perfect foreigner English. "We're very sorry to you, sir. He's from the Belgium, he's not so good on the English. The Belges are a little slow in the head."

"Well if he tries ripping off any more of my shit he'll have a .38 caliber hole in his skull to speed up his stupid fucking thinking. Get the hell out."

We got the hell out. The moment the door closed everyone burst out laughing except me, who was madly sucking down the warm sugar water.

Johnny came up to me. "Hey, you sound like pretty good stupid Belge!"

"Stupid comes natural. I'm from Texas."

We're almost home

If you've never done RR 1431 from Burnet to Austin on a hot March day with the Nordanian national team, it's no use me telling you how manly and epic and heroic it was. But I will tell you this: The sugar rush was so intense that on the first several climbs I rolled to the fore and pushed the pace so hard that Johnny rolled up beside me and said, "Easy, Texas. There's no more sugar water between here and the motel."

They dropped me hard on the giant wall where 1431 widened into four lanes, but I managed to catch back on, and of course they took the hilly route into town through Volente. My apartment wasn't far from the Villa Capri. I peeled off on Speedway, beaten to a pulp. After I recovered, I told the whole story to Fields.

Later that year Fields called me up. "Looks like your training ride got those weakling Danes into shape," he said.

"Oh, yeah?"

"Yeah. John Weltz just got silver at the amateur world road championships. Isn't that the guy you rode with back in the spring on that death march?"

"Yeah! It was!" I hung up the phone and thought about it, not quite sure any more. "Was it?" I said to myself. "Oh, well. It is now."

TINK

I walked in the door, took one look at Mrs. Wankmeister's face, and knew it was bad.

"What are you gonna been doing on my t-shirts drawer?"

"I can explain."

"Lookit at the this one!" She held up two t-shirts, clean ones that were lying on the floor. "And what you gonna say about the that one?" She snatched up another.

"Look, honey, what happened is..."

"I don' wanna hear no 'This honey happened is' poop talk! What are you gonna be saying on the this one? Huh?" Now she had moved to the shorts drawer, and there, spilling out of the drawer and onto the carpet were six or seven pairs of shorts.

"I was finishing up at court, see, and..."

"You ain't gonna do no up court finishing and come home and dump out onna my shirts and shorts! You ain't gonna touch on my shirts and shorts! You been marrying on me twenty-five years and you don' never gone in my clothes drawers!"

"Please calm down! There's no need to shout."

"I'm gonna tell you onna shouting! What is THIS? You gonna tell me on THIS? What's onna THIS?" Now she had moved to the panty drawer, and the holy, untouchable, perfectly folded, immaculately organized panty drawer was now the focus of my attention. "What's a gonna been happening on THIS?"

"It does kind of look like a tornado went through it," I admitted.

"I'm gonna tell on you about some tornado!" she shouted. "That's a my panties drawer! Why you goin' into my panties drawer? You got no business in my panties drawer! I ever gone into your biker tool box with the wrenchy things you don' can't use right and always bustin' stuff so you take it to a bike shop for fixin' and cost a lotta money? I ever mess with that, no I don't! So why you messin' my panties?"

While she caught her breath to get ready for another round of hollering, I seized my chance to explain. "Well, what happened is, Brad and Tink had a bike wreck and got hauled off to the hospital in an ambulance. I was gonna go see if they needed anything."

"What's a Bradandtink?"

"Brad and Tink. They're biker friends."

"Ohhhh," she rolled her eyes. "Itsa dumb biker story again time gettin' all run over on the car."

"No, not by a car. G3 called and said Tink was in the hospital and said 'Can you get some clothes for Tink?' and I said 'Sure.'"

"This Tinks person's a girl or a boy?"

"Tink is a girl."

Mrs. WM's eyes narrowed, which looked pretty gnarly because they were already pretty narrow. "How come you a boy gettin' clothes on a girl? How come she ain't wearin' on her own clothes?"

"She was, but they cut 'em off in the ER because she was concussed and the shorts were shredded from the road rash."

"Why it matters she's a cussin'?"

"Not 'cussin.' Concussion. Knocked out. Blam-o to the head. I went to get her a change of clothes so when she got discharged she'd have something to wear. Simple."

Mrs. Wankmeister looked at me. Her eyes widened as it hit her. The color drained from her face.

"Uh-oh," I thought. "Here it comes."

Here it did indeed come

She wasn't angry anymore. She was in a panic. "You gonna gave on my panties to the girl?"

"Now, before you get all excited, honey..."

"Please don' tell me you gonna gave on my panties to the girl. Please don' tell me onna that. Please don' on the Jesus." She was pleading and on the verge of tears.

"Honey, I went through the drawer and took out a pair at the bottom. They were like, practically brand new. They were so clean and sparkly I had to put on my sunglasses when I held 'em in the light."

That part was actually kind of true. Mrs. WM had a thing about panties being clean enough to eat off of, so to speak.

"What's a color?" I could tell she was racing through her inventory.

"They were kind of gray. Don't worry, honey. I'd never give her those big granny things or the skinny little thong-dealie with the fadeaway in the center."

The mental picture clicked. "They were on a kind of gray with a little pattern speckle, isn't they?"

"Yep. That's the pair."

"I don't ever wore that hardly once or twice."

"See? I checked, honey. They were clean enough to run up a flagpole, or plop out on the desk at a job interview. You're golden. She might not have even worn 'em."

Mrs. Wankmeister cracked a sharp glance. "What kinda girl ain't wearing on underwears?"

"Biker chicks. They're commando half the time anyway. Trust me."

"Oop," I thought. Too heavy on that last one.

"How you gonna know onna biker girls wearin' underpants or not?"

"Uh, well, you can kind of see there's no pantyline when you're riding behind them."

"How come you ridin' behind? You always tellin' me about you're goin' on the fast and can't no one stay on your behind. Now you're tellin' me about a girl's underwear panties line ridin' on her behind?"

"Here, honey," I said. "Let me help you pick this stuff up."

She glowered. "You thinkin' about touchin' on my panties again and we're gonna have to be another big problems."

"Yes, dear," I said, and slowly backed away.

"And next time you're think to givin' onna panties to biker friend girls you can buy a fresher pair onna Target."

"Yes, dear."

Why hadn't I thought of that?

PLEASE DON'T MESS WITH THE DORK WITH THE DORKY SOCKS

Dorky Sock Dude didn't know his socks were dorky. What he did know as he raced along the bike path was that he loved the neon yellow jersey with bright purple sleeves that went flashing by in the opposite direction.

"That," said Dorky Sock Dude, "is the raddest jersey I have ever seen. Where can I get one?"

He had been cycling for about a year and he was proud of himself. He had a new Cannondale. It was bright silver. He had some super rad shifters, Shimano 105. He had an ultra rad helmet with a plastic visor, very pro. And to make it all hang together he had gone out shopping for the best pair of socks he could find, until he found them.

The green and red thunderbolts with orange flames had a black and purple background with yellow asteroids raining down from the top of the cuff. They made him happy every time he pulled them on. They were tall, they were comfy, they were rad, and they were very pro.

The socks totally enhanced how he felt when

he rode, which, from his enthusiasm and the smile on his face was best summed up as "I'm riding my bicycle! Yippee!"

Welcome to the friendly cycling community

Dorky Sock Dude found out that the neon yellow, purple-sleeved jersey he coveted was worn by a certain South Bay cycling club. It was the biggest club. It was the oldest club. It was the most legit club, but Dude didn't know or care about any of that. He wanted the jersey, and he wanted to be teammates with the cool dudes and chicks who wore the cool jersey.

Why? Because bicycle riding was yippee, because he'd been doing it for a year now and thought he was pretty fit, and because anybody who had a jersey that rad must be pretty cool and therefore fun to know.

Dude sent in his membership application and before long he got his jersey in the mail. He was one happy dude. He laid it out on the bed next to his shorts and socks and gloves and shoes and helmet, with his bike off to the side, and admired the ensemble. Dude had done sports in college and he missed being on a team. He felt lucky to have discovered cycling, and even luckier to have learned that there were teams where people could get together to ride and have a good time, and, luckiest of all, that anybody could join.

The next morning he got up, ate breakfast,

and put on his biking duds. He looked at himself in the mirror. He didn't shave his legs like lots of the other bikers he saw, but that's because he didn't understand why shaved legs had anything to do with riding a bike.

Dude had learned that there was a club ride that morning at 6:30 at the Manhattan Beach Pier, the Center of the Known Universe, a/k/a CotKU. He left his house extra early so he wouldn't be late. He felt great and excited and yippee. He'd get to meet his new teammates and they would share workout tips with him and answer some questions that had been bouncing around in his head about cycling and training and fitness and stuff. Mostly stuff.

Nice to see you. Not.

When Dude rolled up to the Pier, there were five or six of his teammates draped nonchalantly on their top tubes, chatting with each other. Dude was so happy he didn't know what to do. They were talking in earnest, so he figured he'd circle around and introduce himself. He was wearing the team jersey and there was no one else in sight, so any minute now they'd nod to him and he'd get to meet his mates.

Nobody said a word to him or even made eye contact. "Wow," thought Dude "they must be talking about serious cycling stuff."

Then, without a word they clicked in and rolled out. Dude hopped on behind the group, hoping someone would say something. They were rolling at a good clip, and occasionally one of the other riders would glance back to see if he was still there.

An unspoken signal was passed and the riders fell into single file, on the drops. Dude was at the end of the line and the pace became hard. He knew it was hard because the other guys were breathing loudly and their bikes started to wobble. "This is cool!" thought Dude. "I guess we're doing intervals now! This is kind of like what we did on the track team in college!"

Dude moved up in the paceline and when it was time for him to pull through he thought, "I better do my turn so they don't think I'm slacking, because it's hard being up there at the front and those guys are gonna want their new teammate to give them some rest!" After a few seconds on the front the riders behind Dude surged past in a straight line, saying nothing, panting hard, beating furiously at the pedals.

"Wow!" thought Dude. "This is great!" He hopped on again the end of the train, which only had three of the original six riders left. Each time it came his turn, Dude pulled through, rotated to the back, then came through again. Soon there was no one left but Dude and one other guy lathered in sweat and making strange choking noises.

They were forty minutes into the ride and no one had yet said a word to him.

Dude got ready to take one final pull. "I'm pretty darn whipped but I'll do this last pull to help

out my teammate behind me. He looks kind of tired."
After Dude took a final hit into the wind and swung
over, he looked back but there was no one left. A
very small group of five riders was far back in the
distance, working together as hard as they could while
Dude continued to pull away. "Shoot!" he said to
himself. "I lost my buddies! NOT COOL!"

Your buddies will be happy you waited

The group caught up to Dude but still no one
said a word. Thinking that Dude was tired, they began
the paceline anew. Within minutes Dude had shelled
the group and was off by himself. "Crap!" he said,
doubly angry because he didn't like to curse, even
silently. "I lost my buddies again! NOT COOL!"

By the third act in the drama the teammates
gave up. Dude had legs of steel and was easily the
match, and then some, of their combined efforts. The
head rider came up to him after everyone had given
up trying to drop Dude. "That Shimano 105 stuff is
total shit," he said.

Dude didn't know what to say. The next rider
pedaled by. "And those socks are dork city. Get some
new socks, man. You look like a clown."

It washed over him. These weren't his
buddies. They'd been trying to ride away from him
but they couldn't. So now the best they could do was
to make fun of his socks and his bike.

To the extent that any of this ever happened,
and I can assure you that all of the true parts really

did, it took place in the late 1990's. And if you've ridden at all in the South Bay, you've met Dorky Sock Dude, otherwise known as G$, otherwise known as one of the best racers in Southern California. He's the one who greets every newcomer with a smile, who encourages every rider regardless of ability, who stops to help you change your flat, who paces you back up to the group, and who, if you race against him, almost always finishes in front. He's the guy that everyone else wants to be like even while he's tearing you a new one.

He's also the guy who wears tall dorky green socks with horizontal black and orange stripes. And the only thing people ask about his footwear nowadays is "Hey, G$, where can I get a rad pair of socks like that?"

NPR

Douggie sent out the word to the South Bay cycling faithful via FB: There would be a new route for the Pier Ride. We'd be axing all the bad stuff including the Marina del Rey death race through the stop lights, the crazy acceleration along Admiralty from a standing start, weaving through the honeycomb of massive cracks in the bad pavement as we spilled into the neighboring lane which was always chock-full of angry commuters, the short but too-long-and-pointless-non-sprunt along Via Marina where the first person to throw up his hands and declare victory got the win, the massive chughole on Pacific that took down VV and left her with enough road rash to bump the stock price for Tegaderm by fifteen percent, the stealth bicyclist killers lurking behind each of the stop signs on Pacific en route back to Washington Boulevard, the semi-pothole right there at the turn back onto Via Marina where, if you weren't careful, you'd smack it and torch a rim, then the hook back onto Admiralty for the true crazy dance of death with gnarly steel plates and their upjutting lips of carnage, the giant ripped up shards of broken pavement, stripped down dirt studded with gravel big enough to chew up a brand new Gatorskin, furious traffic, more stoplights, and the final insane dash back down Fiji Way where it might be Big Steve, or Davy Dawg, or Tree, or Erik, or Hair, or for sure Vapor or some pro who had dropped into L.A. for the weekend, ramping it up to forty mph or maybe forty-five depending on how far off the back you were when the story was being retold at the coffee shop, to the honking finale that, again, no one quite knew where it was, but was definitely there, somewhere, decided again by the first pair of hands to lift off the bars, and then back onto the bike path where you dodged the UCLA knuckleheads blocking the path with sculls, furry-legged bike pathaletes putting the wood to Greg and Marco and Bernard and Eddy and Lance in their dreams and almost colliding with us in the process and of course the low point of all low points, Asshole Number One locking arms with Asshole Number Two walking along the edge of the bike lane as close to us as possible while sticking their elbows out into our faces trying to knock us down as we passed, every single week, then over the steel plate on the bridge where Prez liked to slip, fall, and crack his forehead every now and again, and picking razor sharp oyster shells out of your tires that the gulls had dropped onto the path, through the narrow rebar poles, either one of which if you hit would kill you, back onto Pacific, maybe past the multicolored fatboy Mapei team all the way to the triangle, then left ...

All that was eliminated forever with one simple message on Facebook. Dog bless you, Douggie, because we knew the new route was real when Vapor posted the magic words: "Sounds good to me." Because you know, if it sounded good to Vapor, it was good enough for me, and for you, and you, and you, and you.

And you.

Switching to glide

I timed my departure perfectly. Alarm at 5:30 AM. Slammed the coffee. Slammed the raisin bran. Dashed to the toilet to drop my steaming morning Santorum, along with a couple of smaller Gingriches. Lubed the legs. Pulled on the kit. Danced around for a few minutes as a careless dab of embro put the fire to my balls.

Ratcheted down the Specialized S-Works Pro Road Shoe which, for $360.00, still didn't fit right or stay ratcheted down. Hopped on bike. Noticed rear tire was flat. Threw down bike. Woke up Mrs. Wankmeister with the cursing. Timidly said, "Sorry, sweetie! Nothing! Everything's fine, Snookums!" Cursed some more. Yanked off rear wheel. Yanked out tube. Checked clock. Realized that if not out door in five minutes, no way I would make the ride. Only had one spare tube. Took it out. Partially inflated it. Threw it on floor. Ran into kitchen. Ran back. Noticed old tube and new tube were entangled. Couldn't remember which one was new, which one was flat. Both had a little air in them. Whispered some more "shitfucks" under my breath. Took a gamble and picked the one on top. Stuffed it onto rim. Popped on tire. Grabbed floor pump. Floor pump tipped over, smacked bike, made hellacious racket. Said "Sorry honey sweetums!"

Cursed some more. Pumped up tire. Tube deflated. Ripped out tube. Ripped off another string of oaths. Was "dicksnot" a real cussword? It was now. Put in other tube. Pinched finger. Stabbed palm with plastic tire iron. Ran out of cusswords.

Embro, coffee, and panic had now lathered me into a sweaty, foamy froth. Got tire changed. Aired 'er up. Dashed out the door. Got down to parking garage. Forgot garage door opener buzzer thingy. More gods got damned, mothers fornicated with. Went back upstairs. Went back downstairs. Hopped on bike. Freezing morning air iced everything inside jersey and shorts. Cussed some more. Checked Garmin clock. Ride would leave at 6:40 sharp. Thirty minute ride from the apartment to there. It was now 6:30. Wasn't gonna make it without a time machine. Hammered all the way to Westchester Parkway.

The goose got loose

As I rolled up towards the Parkway, off in the distance I saw the mass of riders approach. I did a U-turn to intercept the pack just as the point of the peloton came rolling through, with Goose Man on the front, all Rapha-ed out in black and nasty pink, to hell with tearing out a page from the Prez fashion manual, he'd taken the whole book.

They let me squeeze in just as Wehrlissimo rolled by, there was Davy Dawg, Big Steve, Tree, G$, Vapor, the Fireman, Tink, Surfer Dan, Hair, Suze, Methuselah Tim, Douggie, and then in a long ragged, panting, sweating, wobbling line there was every wannabe, couldabeen, gonnado, and oughttatry in the South Bay. Instead of the Old Pier Ride, where we just did one loop, the New Pier Ride featured four nasty laps around the Parkway, and I'd caught them at the end of the first lap.

We did the first turn, and Vapor turned up the heat and the popcorn started popping as the wankers, tankers, whackers, and hackers fried off the back. We crested the rise up to the overpass and a yellow city truck came blowing by at fifty, and with the entire left lane to himself decided to get closer and graze the charging peloton, missing me by inches. G$ uncorked an acceleration so hot that the blue stripes on his knee-high SPY hosiery turned green, Wehrlissimo chased and melted, and we made the second turn. I charged off past the light with Flapper Brad and a fellow wanker. The group chased us down and blasted by, with Goose Man leading the charge.

Vapor took over at Turn Three and it was another long line of hurt, misery, despair, desperation, self-loathing, and clawing to stay on the wheel directly in front. The pack had dwindled considerably, with many of the hackers deciding that they'd be more productive at work or on a gurney than out flailing in the middle of this beatdown, and we hit Turn Four. Last time up the hill there was a small break, but I was stuck with the flailers in back and the harder I pedaled the slower I went. The break exploded and the peloton absorbed the broken breakaway.

The final push for the sprunt came, and unlike the Old Pier Ride, where the sprinters were fresh and rosy-cheeked and flexing and ready to wreak havoc, they were for the most part so worked over, tired, and roasted from the four laps of death that they could only watch as Vapor, who could win every one of these wankfests at will but instead preferred to lead out the children to give them a workout, turned on the jets, and with Hair tucked on his wheel and Davy Dawg tucked in behind Hair, Vapor's wheel blew out a contrail of pain and misery and speed so fierce that the only one who could come around was Hair, who switched to glide and pulled away with the victory, the money, the fame, and the glory of being the first ever winner of the New Pier Ride in the history of the world.

Meanwhile, back at the flat

On the last lap I'd hit a rock full force and been forced to do the entire thing, I found out later, on a slowly deflating rear tire. Surfer Dan, G$, and Tink stopped with me after the sprint finish. Dan gave me a tube and assisted with the change. I explained that but for the flat I would have ridden five mph faster than everyone else. They nodded and rolled their eyes.

On the way back we discussed the NPR. Better? Yes. Safer? By far. Roastier? No comparison. Did we plan on going back to the Old Pier Ride once the road crews finished their strip mining project/core to the center of the earth experiment on Admiralty?

Noooooo way.

The Pier Ride was dead. Long live the Pier Ride.

THE TASTE OF BITTER

In nature, few things have been as graced with beauty as the blossom of the pear. In the Golden State, few places look as if they have been repeatedly shot with a large caliber shit pistol so repeatedly as Pearblossom, California.

The town's name came from the multitude of local pear farms along the southern ridge of the Antelope Valley. A few still exist, but most of those farms are now abandoned and have decayed back into the snake-infested desert landscape or have been overridden by tract housing developments, most of which are rotting and empty.

Perhaps it's the first big sign that greets you when you turn onto Pearblossom Highway that says "Dumpsters for Rent!" Perhaps it's the giant billboard in Little Rock that says "We Get You Off!" and shows a picture of a traffic citation with a red strike through it. Perhaps it's the sign announcing a "Gentleman's Club, Opening Soon!" or the paralegal services office in a broken down shack with burglar bars, or the billboard that says "Animals Are Children, Too. Don't Abandon Them!"

The children? The animals?

Maybe it's the signboard for the "opening soon" Pearblossom Fitness Club, or for the torque converters, or the flags of all nations ("Hey, Mom! Let's stop in and get a flag of North Korea!"), signs for used tires, a psychic reader, a thrift store...all the things that are "coming" and "opening soon" juxtaposed with the filthy, broken down, impoverished, trash-strewn, meth-addled community fixtures that already opened long ago to the apparent benefit of no one.

Team Helen's Dev Chicks and Occupy Pearblossom

Fact is, I showed up to this nasty little hell-hole to win a bicycle race. My form had been confirmed at the Vlees Huis road race the week before by none other than Glass Hip, who pulled me aside and said, "Yo, Wanky, you almost didn't suck today. Good job!"

That epic, unforgettable day in the anus of the Central Valley known as Bakersfield, I had had golden legs, or, as Jack from Illinois (not his real name) suggested, "A good enough day of racing to fuel the delusion for another fifteen years that you'll win something."

This morning my veins were chock full of sausage, pancakes, butter, and heavy cream. The stool I had whipped up and deposited in the port-o-potty was not only aesthetically perfect, consisting of a gigantic two-foot long curling brown slug coiled in a nice tight pile and topped with a curly-poop at the end, but its fumes were lethal enough to overwhelm the three gallons of blue chemical roiling the bottom of the turdbox.

It was showtime, and Wankmeister was the show.

And then the Team Helen's Dev Chicks showed up, and all heck broke loose, goshdarnit

Fifteen minutes before my race began, an out of control black SUV careened down to the Positively No Cars Allowed area and tried to run over the sheriff's deputy. "Get your car out of here!" the terrified officer roared.

The Dev Chicks, assuming that they could just drive to the front and get the car valet parked like they did at the Springsteen concert or at Spago, were surprised, but not for long. Gangstachick did a U-turn, ran over $30k worth of bikes, knocked over a porta-potty, and squeezed the SUV into a tiny gravel spot hardly big enough for a Prius.

I pretended not to know them and continued warming up. With ten minutes to go before my race started, Irish Lassie flagged me down. "Oh, dear sweet Wankmeister! We have a mechanical problem. Could you help?"

I was amazed. Not known for my bike mechanic skills, this chick might as well have been asking me to help with her orgasm, another mechanical area where I'd been known to clumsily fumble around unsuccessfully trying to properly adjust tiny, hard-to-see parts to the mutual frustration of all parties concerned. "Uh, sure. I guess. What's wrong?"

"My chain fell off."

"Well, that's easy. Here, let's put the motherfucker back on. I gotta race in five minutes so let's hurry."

Gangstachick paused to watch the proceedings as she pinned on Irish Lassie's number upside down. "Upsidedown, rightside up, who gives a poop? It's not my jersey," she said when the error was pointed out.

Soon, however, Irish Lassie's chaindrop problem became more complex, just as with the female orgasm. The chain had done the impossible — it had fallen off the chainring and then somehow slipped through the chain guard, and now the chain guard was blocking it from being put back up on the small ring. "How the hell did you do that?" I asked. "Put the bike upside down on the bike rack and drive it for three hundred miles over gravel roads and cattle guards?"

Fortunately, Irish Lassie kept her bike well maintained by dousing the chain in two quarts of motor oil before each race. Within seconds, my dainty fingers, and soon my nicely turned wrists, were covered in thick black oil and protective sand. And no matter how many times I shouted "You sorry motherfucker chain guard piece of shit," the chain wouldn't squeeze through the chain guard and onto the chainring. Anyone else would have loosened the chain guard with a hex key and slipped the chain through the widened space, but I preferred brute force and oaths.

Irish Lassie made helpful suggestions such as "I hope this doesn't make you late for your race. You can chase on, can't you?" and "Have you ever put a chain back on before?" and my personal favorite, "Why don't you push it the other way?"

I finally gave up, but not before Gangstachick gave me a blanket that she kept in the back of her SUV next to some pillows for, uh, moving, and I vainly tried to rub off the filthy, oily slime. Suddenly, Irish Lassie cried out "I think I got it!" I turned just in time to see the chain hovering exactly in the perfect position to slip in under the guard. Just like a female orgasm, the impossible was about to happen, but unlike the orgasm, I was actually going to be there to witness it!

"Don't touch it!" I yelled. With a few careful, tender, loving touches, each one gradually increasing in emotion and intensity, the chain finally slipped with a crescendo back under the chain guard and onto the chainring.

Irish Lassie wilted, and Gangstashick wiggled her butt in appreciation.

I raced to the line, my heart pumping, my hands covered in grease, and ready to tear some legs off, or at least put some chains on. Game on!

THE CITY MOUSE AND THE COUNTRY MOUSE

Once upon a time there was a city mouse named Wanky. He was snooty and he thought that Big City was the best place in the whole world. He was even conceited enough to think that one of his local coffee shops was the center of the known universe. He owned a fancy bicycle and only wore bicycle clothing personally designed by his friend, Junkyard Mouse.

Wanky had a poor country cousin mouse from Bakersfield named Lem, who had a cousin named Cletus. Although Lem and Cletus were cousins, like most Bakersfield mice one never inquired too closely as to their consanguinity because it often turned out that "cousin" was a euphemism for "product of an illegal relationship in the lower forty-eight except Texas and Arkansas."

Cultural exchange

One day Wanky called up Lem on the Twitter. "Lem, why don't you come down and do our Donut Ride. You country mice will learn a thing or two about how to ride your bicycles."

"Why thanky, Wanky," said Lem the country

mouse. "That's mighty nice of you. Do you mind if I bring Cousin Cletus?"

"Cletus? Is he the one with the saggy tummy and stumpy tail?"

"That's him," said Lem. "But he would like to come and see what all that Big City riding is like. He don't get out much, except for when him and me get over to Fresno ever now and agin for chain lube and clean underwear."

"How often is that, Cousin Lem?"

"Once or twice a year for sure, whether we need it or not."

"That would be fine," said Wanky. "Be sure to tell him that our Donut Ride is the most glorious ride in Big City. All the Big City mice will be there, as well as one or two Big City rats. They will more than likely gnaw out Cletus's entrails."

Glory or fitness? Glory.

"Will us'n get a good piece of training on your Big City Donut Ride?" asked Lem.

"No," said Wanky. "My third cousin twice removed on Uncle Theodosius's sister's side, Jack from Illinois (not his real name), says that the Donut Ride is the dumbest and worst preenfest of wanker mice he's ever seen. And he's from Hooterville, so he knows a thing or two about wankers."

"Me and Cletus was hopin' for some training."

"We have lots of training in Big City," Wanky said snootily. "You can train with Roadchamp at 3:00

AM and break every Strava record known to mice and men."

"I kinda think we'd like to do that ride," squeaked Lem.

"Only problem is that no one will ever see you. You'll be invisible, eating your pre-ride meal at Peet's Cheeseshop in the pitch dark. You'll have done a hundred and ten miles with eight thousand feet of climbing by the time we even get started on the Donut Ride. Lots of training but no glory."

"What do mean by 'glory'?"

"Glory?" Wanky said with a condescending squeak. "When you roll out on the Donut Ride in Big City, you'll be surrounded by rodentia royalty. The Italian Stallion might even be there."

"Who's that?"

"You might as well ask me 'Who was Ratty?' in the Wind in the Willows," Wanky said. "Or 'Who was Stuart Little?' Or 'Who was Mickey?' Crikey, cousin Lem, the Italian Stallion is the most famous rat in Big City. When he shows up on the Donut Ride, it's Katie bar the door."

All aboard for the Pussy Riot

"Katie bar the door?"

"Yep. Katie Razor will slice you into thin little ribbons of mouse meat and feed you to the pussycats. She did the Leadville 100 walking all the descents and still finished in under four hours. She even carries around an ego bag."

"A what?" Lem's voice quivered on the other end of the Twitter.

"An ego bag. It's a giant bag hooked up underneath her saddle. Bigger than Dallas, even."

"What's it for?"

"She fills it up with all the broken male mouse egos that get shattered on the Donut Ride. Starts the ride empty, goes home full to busting."

"But she's a girl mouse?"

"Not a girl mouse like you have out in the country, Lem. She's a Big City girl mouse. She's pretty, and smart, and well-educated, and knows how to use a napkin, and only blows snot out of her nose when there's no one on her wheel."

"Holy Gouda!" squeaked Lem admiringly.

"But when the hammer comes down, she's the one with her fingers wrapped around the handle of the giant mallet. And it's all the boys whose mice testicles who get whacked."

Lem squeaked in terror. "Are you sure she'll be there?"

"Pretty sure. And even if she's not, Tink will be."

"Who's Tink?" Lem's squeak was so soft that Wanky could hardly hear it.

"She's the climbingest mouse in the South Bay, better even than Katie Razor. Lots of big tough boy mice have tried to pin her in a trap, but the only way to get Tink's attention is to finish with her on the top of a climb. And none of the boy mice have been able to do that yet."

Beware of fools bearing gifts

On the day of the big ride, Lem and Cletus showed up at the Cheese Bean and Cheese Leaf in Big City. Wanky met them and introduced them to much of the Big City royalty. New Mouse was there. Sparkly Mouse was there. Polly Mouse, Douggie Mouse, Jensie Mouse, Gussy Mouse, Junkyard Mouse, Pilot Mouse, G$ Rat, and even Mighty Mouse herself had assembled to greet the out-of-towners.

All mice great and small rolled out, an armada of rodents more than one hundred strong. Even the evil and nasty Big City police cats and Deputy Knox cat were afraid to approach the rolling entourage of cheese eaters.

On the dreaded Switchbacks, the selection occurred with the Italian Stallion, Katie Razor, Tink, John Mouse Hall, and Petey Mouse leading the charge. Lem lasted for a while and was then dropped so badly he was almost fed to the cats. Cletus had his entrails gnawed out. Wanky stalled in no-mouse-land after getting his head caught in a mousetrap after the third turn.

Lem rode well through Better Homes, finished mousefully on the Domes, sprunted well at Hawthorne, and dusted Wanky on the final climb up Zumaya. Cletus was honored at a roadside burial later that afternoon.

Back at the cheese shop in Big City, Lem and

Wanky talked over the day's events. "You Big City mice sure ride hard," said Lem.

"You country mice are no slouches."

"My tail and haunches are pretty sore."

"Wait 'til tomorrow, you'll be even more sore."

"What was that big lake thing on our right the first part of the ride? Was it the Big City sewage pond? Only body of water that big in Bakersfield is the sewage pond."

"It's called the Pacific Ocean, but China calls it their sewage pond."

"Well, someday soon we hope you'll make it up to the country so's we can return the favor. The Big City mice was shore nice to us. That John Mouse Hall feller told me where the turns was, and that Polly Mouse feller did the same thing for Cletus afore he up and died on us."

"I'd like nothing better than to visit you, Cousin Lem. When's a good time?"

"In December the temperature gets down to the low hundreds, which is good because the sewage pond don't smell so rich."

"I'll put it on my calendar."

"And bring some Big City mice with you. We'd like to see if they ride as quick on our roads as they do on yours."

IT DOESN'T SMELL EXACTLY LIKE TEEN SPIRIT

Before you get your ride on you try to clear the tubes, especially after a healthy, high fiber bellyful of bran and yogurt and fruit. There's nothing more awkward than getting thirty miles into a ride up PCH and feeling that knot in your lower gut that says "Fire Torpedo Tube One! Or else!"

Fortunately, I got that "payload knocking at the door" feeling while milling around in front of the coffee shop waiting for the other riders to show. So I hurried in.

Standing next in line for the Starbucks crapper at CotKU on a sunny Friday morning is always an anxious thing. You're there fidgeting because the bran muffin and strong coffee have stomped on the sensors hidden deep in your bowels, and the only real question is whether the person currently in the lockbox is there for a li'l freshen-up or for a seat-clenching full body purge. In my case, the door opened and a plump, middle-aged lady exited. That's usually a good sign because for some reason Manhattan Beach women seem embarrassed by leaving major detonation fumes when there's a line.

Perhaps it's because there's something that conceptually clashes with a $400 pair of yoga pants and a corn-studded, 14-karat bowl buster, or perhaps it's because when they open the door everyone goes, "Eeeeeewwww" and looks them over with what is quite literally the stinkeye. Or perhaps it's just that everyone knows that fully accessorized women don't shit logjams in public.

I stepped into the toilet and immediately realized that the ol' gal before me had dispensed with embarrassment and answered with a hearty "Amen" to what must have been a mighty loud call of nature.

"To hell with you," I thought, "game fucking on." Yes, it would be a battle of the toilet gases, and no chick in a pink leotard was going to overwhelm the mighty issue of my crack if I had any say in the matter. Plus, everyone thinks their own shit smells good, so the sooner I let loose the sooner my vent would overpower hers, or at least neutralize it.

The cranking and rumbling and grumbling that ensued must have struck terror into those waiting outside. Combined with not one, not two, but three industrial flushes that shook the door on its hinges, the poor bastards outside were being put on notice that the next person inside the closet of doom would likely suffer permanent brain damage. With the bran muffin leading the charge I fired off a reverse burping growl-and-plunk that sounded like a logging truck had dumped its cargo off a forty foot cliff into a very deep lake. The folks in line were bathed in a cold sweat.

When I finished, I boldly threw open the door just as a kindly old fellow looked up with a stir stick in his mocha latte. The eyes of everyone in line were glued to my hands, hoping and praying that I'd washed them before touching the handle. I hadn't. The elderly fellow dropped his stir stick as the fumes triggered long repressed memories of mustard gas in the trenches at Passchendaele. I strode proudly out into the sunlight, a spring in my step, five pounds lighter and ready for a fine day in the saddle.

LETTER TO THE EDITOR: WHY I THINK WANKMEISTER IS A DOUCHEY BLOWHARD

It's rare that anyone reads Wankmeister's blog, filled as it is with much sound and fury, signifying nothing. It's rarer still that someone takes the time to dress Wankmeister down for his blustering, mouthy satires that amuse no one but himself, and sometimes don't even do that.

A recent publication of a New Pier Ride recap was met with scorn and derision by one of the mightiest people in the peloton, and someone whose delusions of cycling grandeur occasionally get tangled up with, and therefore become hard to untangle from, reality. Wankmeister can relate!

Below, reprinted sort of with permission but actually probably not, is "The True Unvarnished Unadulterated Unexpurgated Pure Tale of What Really Happened on the Tuesday NPR and Why Wankmeister is a Poser Douchebag but I Love Him Anyway and Can I Have a New Nickname Please?" by Aaron "Hair" W.

So I show up at Telo today and someone says to me, "So Perez beat you in the Pier Ride this morning?". To which I respond, "Hell no! No one was even in the same zip code!". To which they reply, "That's what it said in Seth's blog". My response, "what the fuck is Seth's blog!?". So I read it for the first time tonight ...dude, you are one bad ass writer! But your killing me with the whole, "Me have big swinging dick, me take so many pulls". It's redundant, and people are just gonna tell you to stop whining. So let me help ya out with the taking a pull thing ...if your taking that many pulls, your not pulling hard enough. When I take a pull, it's to break mother fuckers off. It ain't to keep the pack speed at some certain average speed. People don't respond well to hard accelerations ...and that's what I like to give them. And if it don't break shit up, well, it took all the pop out of their legs for the finish. So change the mantra ...fuck pulling, attack bitches! Attack over and over and over until we break the bitch in two!

Now let me give you the final finish, since it seems you were unable to pull through that section ;) At the turn around by Sepulveda, 5 Big Orange guys got off the front, and Leibert sat in front of Derek, Mark-Paul (our other teammate), and myself to block. This part is comical ...even with Leibert soft pedaling, these guys were not pulling away. So I said to Leibert, "Tell them you can't go any slower!" ...I could see Leibert was disappointed.

Anyhow, Derek, MP, and myself took over at the top of bridge before Loyola and were on the front all the way to the finish. And when the sprint happen, I can assure you Perez was nowhere near me (or in front of me for that matter). So reprint that shit bitch! ;) And tell these weak dick mother fuckers to start attacking more! When the group slows up, it's cause their hurt'n ...so fuck'n hit 'em again!

Now don't get all teary eyed, and take any of this shit personal ...cause you big dick swings too low for that.

And for Christ Fucking Sake, come up with a better fucking name than "Hair" ...maybe something like,

"Giant Swinging Dick" or "Totem Poll Dick!
...you're one of my favorite dudes, seriously.
and thanks for all the other compliments in some of your post.

-AaronW (GSD)

Now I know what you're all thinking. "Does he have any idea how hard people are going to laugh when this goes up on the Internet?" and "Does he even know what the Internet is?" And I can answer that for you: "No, and no, but he soon will."

So, it has now become necessary for Wankmeister to defend his honor, and since he has none, he will go and borrow someone else's for a few minutes. So listen up, Hair.

You've broken a bunch of rules with this noxious missive, which is awesome. You are fast and smart and tough and you train hard and you win races (I'm making that last part up). But there are some rules that even you can't get away with breaking. Here they are:

1. Don't ever ask for a nickname. Nothing good will come of it, ever. Just ask the dude who wanted to be nicknamed "Cheap Trick" and is now known as "Nancy."

2. Don't ever ask for a "better" nickname if one has already been bestowed. It's like being a crippled dude with syphilis and telling people not to call you "Gimpy." The only possible replacement is going to be worse, unless you've always fancied being called "Skankdick."

3. No matter what, don't ever, ever, ever (and you can toss in a couple more "evers" for emphasis) tell anyone what you really want to be called. Especially me. It will make the consequences of #1 and #2 above look positively benign.

So you've fucked up, and now you're going to be punished. Henceforth you shall only be known as Super Heroic Radically Impressive Manly Penis Yeoman Doing Incredibly Crazy Kermesses. But since that's a mouthful and takes too long to type, we're just going to call you by the acronym. Or, we could go back to using "Hair." Your call, buddy.

Nicknamedly,
Wankmeister

PS: After you get through strumming that totem pole, go the front you sandbagging wanker.

CROWN JULES

All year I'd been hearing about Jules. It usually went like this.

> Wanker: Some little kid showed up on the Donut Ride and kicked everyone's teeth in.
>
> Me: Huh?
>
> Wanker: Yeah. Little twelve- or thirteen-year-old kid. Rode everyone off his wheel.
>
> Me: Yeah, right.
>
> Wanker: I'm serious.
>
> Me: Twelve years old? No way.
>
> Wanker: That's what we thought. No way a little kid would have the lungs for that kind of sustained effort.
>
> Me: Not possible.
>
> Wanker: Why don't you come out and see for yourself?
>
> Me: I'm busy that week.
>
> Wanker: Which week?
>
> Me: Whichever.

The overture

I rolled out this particular morning knowing that the sunny weather and beautiful skies would mean a huge turnout for the world famous South Bay

Donut Ride. Surfer Dan, Derek the Destroyer, and several other big hitters were there, though, so it was going to be hard.

"Hey Dan, see that kid?"

"What kid?"

Jules was so short that he was invisible off on the edge of the peloton. "That one up there with the national champion shorts."

"Yeah. What about him? What's he doing here?"

"He's going to ride away from everyone in this hundred-man group once we hit the Switchbacks with the exception of about seven dudes. Everyone else will be put to the sword and have to go home today and say 'I got my ass handed to me by a thirteen-year-old.'"

Dan gave me that look as if to say, "You are a fool, fool." But instead he just said, "Really?" He's a polite dude.

"I know it sounds crazy. Just watch. He's gonna run a hot poker up the ass of every tender, middle-aged ego out here. You'll see."

Up, down, and around the bend

I watched Jules for a couple of minutes, marveling. He navigated the pack with ease and skill. Giant men on giant bikes bounded by him, around him, and in front of him with all the kookish bike moves that infest the Donut Ride at every turn of the pedal once you get more than ten wheels back. Jules expertly avoided the freds and then drilled it up the edge of the road, rocketing into a solid position behind Dan as we climbed out of Malaga Cove.

At age twelve he knew more about finding good wheels and staying there than I did at fifty.

I wondered why no one was talking to him. Here was a kid with the confidence, skills, and proven ability to go out on a big boy's ride and smash people's heads in. This wasn't just precocious, it was pre-precocious. "Maybe," I thought, "you wankers should talk to him and get to know him now, before he starts peering out at you from magazine covers."

"Hey, man, what's your name?" I asked.

"Jules," he said sounding totally cool and totally grown up.

"I'm Seth. Nice to meet you."

Brief smile. "Yeah."

He told me about his recent trip to Trexlertown, where he scored some impressive results on the track. The track explained his great bike handling. A bit of pre-ride research had shown that Jules was an omnivorous cyclist. He races track, crits, road, time trials, and 'cross, and is good in every single discipline. His long string of firsts and seconds from 2011 were briefly depressed in 2012 as he had moved into the next age bracket, but his winning trajectory being what it was, that would take care of itself in the next year or two.

Calm before the storm

No one wanted a hard approach to the Switchbacks that morning so it was a big, lummoxing group as we rolled up Lunada Bay and into Portuguese Bend. At the beach club, where the pace is often single file, the ride continued its leisurely pace. I heard riders chatting behind me, a giveaway for the ease of the ride. On a hard day the only sound would be labored, choking breath, most usually my own.

Of course, an easy run-up to the Switchbacks meant that the actual climb would be exponentially faster, as people would have fresh legs when the climb started. A couple of attacks went off past the beach club, but it wasn't until G$ opened up the throttle that the ride began in earnest.

G$ dragged a small contingent of seven riders all the way to the base of the climb, then swung over. The pack was a tiny speck far behind. Just before cresting the first flat spot on the climb, shortly after beginning the next section climb, I blew. The six riders in the break rolled off. As I dropped back into a rhythm I heard the sound of an approaching bike.

It was Jules.

Are you a grown man? Do you have an ego? Do you consider yourself fit? Have you ever thought that "but for" you'd have been a pro? Is your weekly slugfest a validation of your ability and strength? If you've answered "yes" to any of these questions, then the realization that you're hanging for dear life onto the wheel of a barely-turned-thirteen-year-old child will devastate you.

Though he provided precious little draft it was enough to latch on, and this kid proceeded to take out his bullwhip, inspect the tip to make sure the knot was properly tied, and beat the snot out of me with it. He had his eyes glued on the break and would periodically get out of the saddle to jam it even harder.

We overtook Rico Suave from Big Orange, who jumped on my wheel. I blew after the first hairpin as Jules got out of the saddle again and lit it up. Suave, an experienced racer, hunkered down and let Jules pull him for quite a way until he could recover, then he attacked the kid and dropped him. Nice.

I kept Jules in sight until the final turn, and then he was flat out gone. By the time I rounded the last corner he had already reached the top of the hill and I never saw him again. Of course the short tow I'd gotten from this dynamo had put me so far ahead of the chasing peloton that I had time to overhaul my bottom bracket by the time the next shattered group rolled up.

So if, a few years from now you hear the name "Jules," and it's spoken with a trembling voice tinged with fear and awe, don't say you weren't warned.

CONFESSIONS OF A DIRTY RACER

I've been racing dirty.

There. I said it.

The signs have been out there for a while, but I thought people wouldn't connect the dots, especially since I've been such a vocal advocate for clean cycling. But the thing that pushed me to confess, aside from my conscience, was an email from a friend. "It doesn't add up, dude. Why don't you come clean?"

The "it" he was referring to was a series of eyebrow-raising results, starting with a CBR crit at the end of last year where I got tenth out of a break that included some phenomenal competition. Then, I finished Boulevard with the group. Typically I get dropped on the first lap. Next was a third place crit finish, 50+ CBR. Icing on the cake was third place, also at a CBR race, where I overplayed my hand by riding in every break and collecting three primes.

Now that I've confessed, I'm going to do what others who've been caught most often refuse to do. I'm going to explain how an older masters racer goes from racing clean to racing dirty. It's not a pretty story.

The problem is, of course, rooted in my childhood

When I was a little kid I hated taking baths. Getting me wet and soaped down was always what my mom called a "production." After cajoling, threatening, chasing, and finally manhandling me into the tub, a process that took a solid hour and that was utterly exhausting to a woman with already frayed nerves, once I was in, I was equally hard to get out.

My brother and I would have water wars, spill most of the tub water onto the mildewy tile, and leave the porcelain claw-footed bath with a thick black grease ring that took a can of Ajax and a bad case of elbow tendinitis to remove. If she could get me bathed twice a month it was a victory. In the summertime the success rate was even lower.

Why was I such a dirty little kid? Because I was from Texas, because we didn't have a TV, because I was always outside, because I was always barefoot, and because of Fletcher.

When there's a funny smell, blame it on the dog

Fletcher was our mixed German Shepherd - Airedale - Snipsnsnails mutt who rescued us when we went to the La Marque ASPCA to get adopted by a pet. Fletcher grew up into a rather large mammal, and like every dog in Texas from his generation, that meant he hosted a large population of fleas.

Yes, dogs used to have fleas. There were no magical flea collars or special flea-icides that you rubbed into their coat, and there sure weren't any mobile mutt washers painted pink with names like

"Poochy Pedicures" or "Doggie Style."

In those days the only way to kill the fleas was with a garden hose and a box of flea powder made by DuPont or Dow that contained a chemical so strong it would make your fingers rot off or dissolve the enamel on your teeth when you added it to the bathub gin, but that never, ever killed one solitary flea.

Instead, the lethal flea powder made the fleas stronger, bigger, jumpier, and it supercharged their flea libidos such that after the flea bath Fletcher would, within days, have twice as many fleas as he did before the rubdown. Since Fletcher slept in my bed and on the couch, and since I played with him on the floor, and in the grass, and in the mud, I, too, was covered in fleas.

Many was the lazy summer afternoon when my brother and I would sit on the formerly white couch that had become brown and catch fleas, expertly laying them on their side, up against the hard edge of our fingernails as we popped them in half for having the audacity to bite us. Fletcher was indeed a filthy, dirty dog, but not just because of fleas.

He was especially nasty because he was constantly licking his balls. Nowadays the first matter of business when you get a dog is to whack off his gonads, but not in 1968. Dogs in those days had balls, and big dogs had big ones. Dogs grew to maturity with their nuts intact. Fletcher's balls were big and purple and of all his body parts, they were the ones that never got bitten by a flea. He licked and slurped and kept those things scrupulously clean, and woe betide the flea who tried to suck the blood out of either of those big doggie nuts. Whatever else you could have said about Fletcher, you couldn't question his priorities.

In addition to constantly licking his balls, Fletcher would often lick us boys as well, on the hands if we were eating something, on the face if he saw a bit of peanut butter that hadn't made it down the gullet, or on the legs if he just needed some salt. So I grew up, in addition to having fleas, with a layer of dirty dog slime that covered me from head to toe.

As a side note, and in confirmation of what recent studies suggest about the link between childhood illness and playing in filth, suffice it to say that I never got sick.

When the boy becomes a man

I cruised through Braeburn Elementary School a dirty and greasy urchin and never thought much about it. Then, one day in seventh grade we were sitting in the cafeteria at Jane Long Junior High and the guys started talking about bathing. It was 1978, and boys had long hair.

First was Danny Martin, who had long, black, shimmering, beautiful hair. "When do you shower?" he asked Steve Wilson, who had long, shiny bronze hair.

"Before school, for sure."

"Me, too," said Danny.

Bill White, who had long, silky, blonde hair, piped up. "I shower at night, too. But I only shampoo in the morning."

Everybody looked at me, including Glynis Wilson, the lovely girl with the gorgeous long hair. I stammered. "Uh, only in the, uh, morning."

A fiery curtain of red started at my neck and enveloped my entire head as I realized I couldn't even remember the last time I'd bathed. In my entire life I'd never showered. That was for girls. Then I looked at Glynis and a light went on. Maybe girls weren't so bad.

If I could have covered my head in a bag the rest of the day, I would have. I rushed home and ran to the bathroom. There, staring out at me from the mirror was an oily face topped with a rat's nest of long, thick, matted, greasy hair. I jumped in the shower. I washed my hair, I washed off the fleas, I washed off the dog slurp, and I never intentionally missed a morning shower for the next thirty-six years.

Racing clean

When I started racing my bicycle in 1984 I raced clean, and I believe that most of the peloton did, too. There was always the dirty racer here and there, but for most of us there were too many compelling practical reasons to stay clean.

First and foremost were the shorts. Word was that if you wore the same shorts for even two days running you'd end up with butt boils and ass chancres and festering saddle sores the size of a fried egg. That scared us, so we washed ourselves and we washed our shorts.

Second of all was the stink. We were young men and we smelled rather badly rather quickly. Unlike the halcyon years of little boydom, when I could go unbathed for weeks and never smell much worse than a mild case of mildew, all that changed with puberty.

Any mom who's opened the closed door of a teenage son's room knows this smell. It's the dank, rank, febrile, fertile smell of boymones, those chemicals that lace everything they touch with the strong odor of reproduction. Stick a young man on a bike and make him pedal around in the hot Texas sun for a few hours, and you'll wind up with a case of the serious stinks, the noxious body odor that screams "I'm in France!" or "Next we invade Rome!"

So between the stink and the sores it didn't make sense to race dirty, and I didn't. For over thirty years I rode clean.

When the levee breaks

I have to admit that it was frustrating, especially as I got older, slower, weaker, and more stupid. People who had once begged for mercy on my mighty wheel now came around me barely cracking a sweat. Was I that slow? Had my decline in my forties been that rapid? Was that massive sucking sound at the end of every chain gang me?

I tried everything. Diets. Power meters. I once spoke with a coach. I even talked to a guy who knew someone who had been properly fitted on a bike. I traded in steel for carbon. Wool for lycra. I buried myself in the physics and metrics of performance with the singular goal of cycling success. But the only compromise I refused to make was riding dirty. I'd win clean or I'd not win at all.

But then I'd look around and see some dude who wasn't nearly as experienced, who didn't train nearly as hard, and he'd spank me without even trying. I knew those guys were dirty and I finally decided, if just to prove it to myself, that if I were as dirty as they, then I could win, too.

The long descent into corruption

The first thing I learned about racing dirty is that you don't get fried egg-sized saddle sores. That's just a fairy tale they use to scare away the goody two-shoes and keep them from going to the dark side. I found that you could wear the same pair of shorts three, four, five times (six if you were Brad House), with no ill effects.

Riding dirty wasn't so bad and the cash you saved on laundry could go straight to gas money and entry fees. That's how the corrupt system works, giving dirty riders a financial advantage. It's sad, but true.

The other big fear riders have about riding

dirty is that they'll smell bad. This is true for the young dudes, but old fellows lose the stink of youth starting about age forty, and by fifty the testosterone odor has been completely replaced by Ben Gay. You can sweat for days on end and go to bed with a salt crust encasing your entire skin and it will only barely out-duel the smell of your joint creams and diaper balms.

In short, I got on the dirty racing program and it worked. Even though I didn't smell that bad, it was bad enough for guys not to want to draft off me, or at least not to draft too closely. And once I knew the secret I could immediately tell who else was riding dirty and who was riding clean. That's how it was when I was on the program and it would shock you to hear some of the big names that were on it, too.

Anyway, I've tried it and I've had enough. It's time for Mrs. WM to let me move back in from the porch. From now on I'm going back to riding clean. But if there's real money or prestige on the line, you never know...

NO CHOPPING, PLEASE

New Girl rolled up beside me on the Wheatgrass Ride. "Can I ask you something?" She has fallen headfirst into the Kool-Aid vat, and when she's not racking up new QOMs on Strava she's hanging out at all the après-ride coffee klatsches.

"Sure."

"So I've got a wheel on the Parkway yesterday at the end of the NPR, and it's leading up to the sprint, and some guy grabs my arm and pushes me off the wheel. What am I supposed to do? I almost crashed. It really scared me."

"Well, New Girl, that's a very good question. Since you're new to the group and people aren't familiar with you yet, you need to approach this kind of thing delicately, with diplomacy and humility. Who was it?"

"I'm not sure. Some guy I've never seen before. I was trying to stay upright."

"The next time it happens, make a note of who it was, and then ride up to him after the sprunt and introduce yourself. Meekness is key. 'Hello, I'm New Girl, and I'm new at riding, and this group ride is new for me, and I want to apologize for bothering you.' That kind of thing."

She listened, but didn't like the subservience.

"Then, when you've got his attention, you want to politely — and I can't stress how important this is — point out that he bumped you hard while you were on a wheel and that it frightened you, and was perhaps a bit unsafe and not very sporting."

"Yes?'"

"Yeah. Then say to him in your sweetest voice, 'Listen, if you ever touch me again I'm going to rip your tiny little balls off by the roots and stuff them down your throat.' Then elbow him in the ribs, or head-butt him, or chop his wheel to show him you mean business. If he crashes out and splits his skull on the pavement, spit into the bleeding cranium for emphasis."

New Girl's eyes got wide because she saw I meant it. "I can't do any of that stuff."

"Fine. Come tell me, or Iron Mike, or Davy Dawg, or Fireman, or Junkyard, or any of your buddies. We'll not only tell the jackanape, we'll bust his chops."

It's like a penis, only smaller

Women who ride in the pack, especially on the Donut Ride or the NPR, have it doubly tough. First they have to do the actual ride. On fast days, it can be a challenge to hang on no matter who you are, let alone stay among the first five or ten wheels where it's safest. Even slow days have several "points of interest" where there's an attack, or a sprunt, or an extended hard surge.

And let's not kid each other. It's physically hard to compete with the fastest people on these rides. Nor should we kid ourselves about something else. The women who show up and hang are a thousand times tougher than most of the guys. Many of the South Bay local biker chicks are marathoners, ex-pros, full time professional trainers, former Olympians, and general badass athletes who are already better than a huge chunk of the men anyway. But in addition to competing with the men, the women who do the group rides in the South Bay have to contend with something much harder than the physical demands of the ride, which are strenuous enough. They have to contend with the dreaded TPS, otherwise known in the medical literature as Tiny Pecker Syndrome.

Every woman has experienced it. She's pounding along, minding her own business, moving up in the pack or passing people on the climb, when she moves ahead of Lucius Lardbottom, he of the exquisitely tiny pecker. He's flailing, he's at the end of his rope, and in his case the fat lady not only sang but has gone home and taken a leisurely hot bath. He's flat fricking done.

But lo! The minute that the fit biker chick cruises by, Lucius gets a new lease on life, inspired as if by Dog himself. Why? Because no chick is gonna pass him on his bike!

He jerks up on the pedals, swerves dangerously, and mashes down with a ferocity that surprises the chick, who was minding her own business and focused on riding her bike. Lardbottom glares, he pants, he lunges, he beats his meaty ass up and down on the saddle as if engaged in a new butt-tenderizing posture. Spittle comes out in a thick spray and his breathing evokes the death shudder of a beached ocean mammal. The chick is taken aback but keeps coming, and he becomes a hazard to himself, to her, and to everyone else on the road. The future of the universe depends on not getting passed by the chick, and he'll do anything to prevent the inevitable.

He'll bump her. He'll swerve across her wheel. He'll reach out and push her off the wheel if she's lining up for the sprunt. And he'll do this and a thousand other chickenshit maneuvers when, if the passer had been a man, he would have simply continued his implosion and nodded as he mutely acknowledged the superiority of the other guy.

Eventually, though, Lardbottom blows and fades away. If the syndrome is this pronounced on training rides, the women who race with the men in the CBR crits have it even worse. The many men afflicted with TPS are galled that a woman would dare show up and try to beat them on race day, despite the fact that they do exactly that.

Try to show a little respect

Women who do the group rides don't deserve to be cut any slack, or to be given a helping hand, or to be coddled like lumps of sugar when the hammer comes down. That's not what they're in it for. But they do deserve the same respect and fair treatment accorded to the guy whose jock you're so desperately trying to sniff. If you find yourself locked in mortal combat trying to beat one of the women on the ride, kudos to them for stretching your neck and props to you if you're riding safe and fair. But if you're chopping wheels so you don't get beaten by a chick? Not cool.

When I first started doing the Old Pier Ride I had my ass handed to me on a plate by Cupcake. She had my wheel and I tried to ride her off it, not because she's a woman, but because I was intent on winning the sprint against all comers, her included. Her bike handling skills are a thousand times better than mine, she's ten times tougher and a whole lot savvier. When I blew she sailed by as if I were standing still. It never would have occurred to me to change my line or to bump her as she passed, or to do anything other than recognize that I'd been whipped by my betters.

And while I don't like getting the snot beaten out of me, I'd never think about holding it against the person who did it fair and square through superior riding, whether a guy or a chick or a fifteen-year old kid, which is a good thing because I've been stomped by them all.

WE GOT YOUR BACK!

The first time I heard the patrol car bleep his horn, we were headed towards the turn to begin the last lap on the NPR. "We'll be seeing him again," I thought.

Lap Four played out in all its glory: Vapor leadout, Hair spanking all pretenders in the sprint, and the Prez making a last-minute acceleration from too far back but almost taking the win thanks to his pink gloves, green socks, and purple helmet. We reached the red stoplight at Pershing and the cruiser pulled up next to us. The cop was unhappy. "Who's the leader of this ride?" he yelled.

Each of the seventy riders knew that the first person to answer this question would in effect be saying, "Write ME the ticket, officer." So no one said anything.

"That's okay," I thought. "I'm surrounded by my crew. There's nothing that one cop can do against this phalanx of mighty warriors." So I hollered back at him. "I'm not the leader, but I'd be more than happy to talk with you."

"Pull over there!" he ordered as the light turned green.

We seventy badasses aren't scared of no damn cop

I pulled into the turnout and dismounted,

confidently approaching the policeman. Well, it was more deferentially than confidently. My father had always said that the only proper answer to a person in a bad mood with a badge, a gun, and a pair of handcuffs was "Yes, sir."

"You guys can't ride like that," he said.

"Yes, sir."

"You're spilling out from the far right lane and filling up the entire second lane as well. It blocks traffic and is incredibly dangerous."

"Yes, sir."

"Look, I respect what you all are doing out here. You're in great shape, you're doing a healthy workout, and that's good. We have no problem with that. But when you block the entire road, someone's going to get hurt."

"Yes, sir."

"Now, what's your name?"

"Perez. Dave Perez."

"Okay, Mr. Perez. What's your phone number?"

"It's, uh, 867-5309. Area code 310."

The cop looked at me funny. "I've heard that number before."

"It's, uh, common, sir."

"I'm not going to cite you, but I'd appreciate it if you got the word out to the folks in your club that you can't block both lanes."

"Yes, sir."

"I've talked to this group before. What's the

name of your club? South Bay something?"

"Yes, sir. South Bay Wheelmen? No, we're not a club. This is just an unorganized ride. It's..."

"Look, I know you guys are a club and this is a club ride. Which club is it?"

"Yes, sir. But sir, we're a bunch of different clubs." I held up my SPY armwarmers. "I ride for team SPY. And all these other people," I jerked my hand over my shoulder, "ride for various clubs. There are people from all over the U.S. and the world, and even Australia, who join on this ride."

I was thankful that Caveman James from Colorado had joined us, as I could pull him out from the throng as proof that we weren't just one big club ride but rather an amalgamation of unrelated idiots, some of whom were not far removed from Paleolithic Man. Caveman had his best American Flyers full Russian facebeard and really did look like a foreigner or a space alien.

The cop was scowling. "Why's everyone wearing the same outfit then?"

"Same outfit? There are at least a dozen different..." I turned around to start pointing out the different kits and teams who were represented on the ride, but stopped mid-sentence. The massive gang of supporters had melted away. No one remained but Sparkles, New Girl, Haunches, and a couple of other wankers who had stayed to watch the cuff and stuff. The only team kits were Ironfly and, of course, South Bay Wheelmen.

"Mr. Perez, those outfits clearly say South Bay Wheelmen."

"Yes, sir. I can explain, sir."

"I'm sure you can. Just like I can write you a ticket."

"Yes, sir."

"But I'm not going to," he continued. "I'd like you to get the word out. We want this to be safe just as much as you do. If it spreads out into a long line because you're going fast, so be it. But when things bunch up and start blocking both lanes we're going to intervene."

I couldn't explain that he'd seen us just before the turnaround, and that with few exceptions we did a good job of stopping for lights, stopping for oncoming cars, checking before we U-turned, and being safe except for the last four hundred yards when people risked everything, especially the lives of their friends, for the glory of winning the sprint. "Yes, sir."

"And what's with those socks?"

"These, sir?"

"Yeah. Why the tall pink socks?"

"It's ah, breast awareness, sir."

"Excuse me?"

"Cancer, I mean. Breast cancer awareness. Think pink breast awareness," I mumbled, blushing.

"Okey-dokey." He shrugged. "You guys and gals be safe out there, okay?"

"Yes, sir," I said.

"Now go catch up with your group. Have a good day, Mr. Perez."

"Yes, sir!" We looked at each other, knowing full well that everyone was already back at CotKU quaffing their third latte and taking bets on who had gotten the ticket.

New Girl clapped me on the back as we remounted. "Coffee's on me, Wanky, or should I say 'Mr. Perez?' Thanks for taking one for the team."

"Oh, it was no big deal. He wasn't going to give me a ticket."

"How did you know that?"

"I've already gotten one this year. That's my limit. Now if this had happened in 2013, I'd never have volunteered to be the one to talk to that cop."

She rolled her eyes. "I'm buying your coffee anyway."

ON BEATING RICHARD THE UNMEEK

Every pre-race team meeting by every masters team in Southern California began with the same question. "How're we gonna beat Richard the Unmeek?"

Everyone would then stand around and draw circles in the dust with their big toe like the mice in Aesop's "Belling the Cat."

"Let's attack him early and win out of a break."

"He always marks those attacks."

"Let's take him with us in the break, then."

"He can outsprint anyone in the break."

"Let's chase all the breaks, including his, and lead our guy out for a field sprint."

"He always wins the field sprint. He's the current crit national champion."

"Let's let him dangle off the front then run him down towards the end when he's all tired from working solo, and then crush him in the sprint."

"We tried that at the state road race, remember? He was off the front for forty-five miles, we brought him back and he still won."

After this type of conversation everyone generally goes out and races and gets beat. By Rich.

The secret to beating the Unmeek in a crit

This particular day we learned that the secret weapon to keep Rich from winning was by getting to the guy who glues on his front tire. If you could get to that guy you suddenly had a chance.

The Brentwood Grand Prix takes place at the galactic center of hot chicks, fake boobs, guys in Ferraris, Schwarzeneggers, the Simpsons (O.J. *and* the comic strip voiceovers), and the full-on West L.A. vibe.

Is your region's signature event in a place called Hooterville? Is your best crit of the year in an office park? Ours isn't.

Brentwood GP happens along a tight, technical little course with a couple of grinding bumps, a fast tailwind, a hard headwind, and oh-shit turns that test your ability to actually handle a bike. There's always at least one guy in any crit who is so terrible, jerky, sketchy, twitchy, and unable to control his bike that I'm terrified throughout the race to be anywhere near him. To make matters worse, that guy is usually me.

The Hatchetman, our strategy guru, chaired the team pre-race planning session. "We got seven guys. Nails won San Marcos last weekend convincingly. If we play our cards right we can get him the win in this one, too."

"What about the Unmeek?" I asked.

"Here's the plan. Wanky, you will get dropped

after the first couple of laps, after which the official will pull you from the race so you can detail my car while you're waiting for the race to finish. But until then we need to make maximal use of your two hundred watts of incredible power. When the gun goes off, hit the front and string it out."

"Then what?"

"It will give you a chance to crash on the first or second turn before people have gotten too tired to avoid you. Tats, Fritos, Critboss, and I will stay towards the front, cover any moves, and keep Nails in position in case the Unmeek rolls off."

"How's Nails gonna beat the Unmeek?" I asked.

Several dudes glowered at me.

"Then, with two or three to go, we'll get Critboss up into position for the finish, along with Nails if he's not off the front."

"But what about..."

I never finished the question and my teammates sped off to the line.

Breaking bad. Really, really bad.

The race started at a torrid pace, with everyone diving for the first turn, which was a 180-degree pivot that went up a little bump and then drove down through a chicane and onto a wide straightaway. As we went through the first turn I heard behind me the grinding, skidding, cursing, smashing, banging, whanging, panic-inducing sound of some wanker falling on his ass.

The sound scared me so badly that I jumped hard and raced away, dragging the pack behind me for a solid forty or fifty amazing yards. As I swung over, the Unmeek came through breathing fire and hand grenades at a speed normally reserved for things with large internal combustion engines.

Fifteen minutes into the fifty-minute event I was hauling through the start-finish with Hatchetman in hot pursuit of a fifty dollar prime. Kalashnikov, who needed gas money just as badly as I did, powered by with a hard surge. "Fuck," I thought. "He can have the money, because I got cheered by Irish Lassie, who distinctly yelled 'Dig deep, Wanky!' as I zipped through the turn before the finish. Winning!"

I had wanted to tell her that if I dug any deeper I'd be in China, but the shortage of oxygen in the Brentwood area made that impossible.

The peloton paused after Kalashnikov took the prime and I rocketed fifty slots back to check on some of my good friends and make sure they were okay. One of them was a dude in a black kit with a giant red license tag hanging from his seat rails that said "Handicapped." Some things even I can't make up.

The Unmeek then "rolled off the front," which is what people say when someone jacks away from the peloton so hot and hard that you couldn't catch them even if you offered a prime of hookers and blow. It was classic Unmeek: You take the prime,

I'll take the race victory.

They don't make Yugos any more

This was the critical moment in every race where the contenders, the wannabes, the couldabeens, the oughtahaves, and the shouldacouldas had to either man up, put their heads down and close the gap in the teeth of a headwind or do what bike racers do best: Look at each other and say, "You go!"

To which the other dude says, "Fuck that. You go."

By which time the thirty mph gap means you will have to go thirty-two mph without the cozy protection of all the people whose wheels you've been sucking for the entirety of the race if you want to bridge to the leader.

Nails, never a fan of the Yugo, instead hopped into his Igo and bridged. Kalashnikov tried, but was winded from his gas money effort. Various other riders tried but in a flash Hatchetman and the Unmeek's teammate, Glass Hip, came to the front and began doing efforts that were just slower than the break, allowing the leaders to establish and then build on their gap, but still fast enough that no one wanted to chase.

Although the gap yo-yoed, at one point getting down to ten seconds when the Ironhead and his merry band of assassins tried to close the gap, the constant teamwork of SPY and Amgen, and the iron legs of Nails and the Unmeek meant that the break succeeded.

With five laps to go I knew it was my turn to move to the front so I could help with a last lap lead-out. I sprunted down the straightaway as hard as I could, using my last ounce of power, and in a flash had moved up from 76th to 73rd. The only thing that remained was for the Unmeek to beat Nails for the win and for someone else to take the field sprint.

When tires go bad

On the bell lap, however, a miracle happened. The closer, the state road champ, the state crit champ, the national crit champ, the badass who doesn't just bring home the bacon but brings home the entire pig, Richard the Unmeek himself came red-hot into the penultimate turn and rolled a tire.

Fortunately, although Rich was five pounds lighter from the skin loss, he wasn't badly hurt. Even more fortunately for us, it meant that our closer, Nails, got to roll across the start-finish first, hands held high in victory.

HOW TO MAKE FRIENDS IN AMERICA

Dear Fellow with the Funny Accent,

It was a pleasure meeting you on our world famous Donut Ride this morning. I was sitting a couple of wheels behind you as we rolled past Terranea. The Velo Pasadena dude in front of you moved over to the left. You weren't paying attention, and you swerved wildly even though all that was required was a gentle change of line.

The riders behind you yelled in the typically friendly way we Americans greet our foreign guests on densely packed, amped-up flailfests like the Donut Ride. One fellow said something like "Hey fucktard! Watch what the fuck you're doing!"

Another friendly greeting was also sent your way, something along the lines of "Hey! You almost took me out, ya fuggin' kooktard!"

It was our subtle way of saying that your maneuver had imperiled others, some of whom had jobs (okay, that's stretching it), but all of whom had plans for later in the day that didn't include a fractured skull. So far it was just a bit of banter on the morning ride.

But things went south when instead of

looking back sheepishly and saying "Sorry, mate, I'm a kook," you went on the offensive and began blaming your flail on the Velo Pasadena dude. Now I know you've only been in this country for a short while and it's likely that your former prison colony doesn't celebrate cycling quite the way we do, but the little stars on that dude's sleeve meant that he's a former national champion.

Again, no big deal except that when you, a kooktard with a bad attitude and poor handling skills, blame your flail on a dude who is at least allegedly the best in the nation at his craft, then you look like an even bigger kooktard crazypants. "So piss off!" you're probably thinking.

How do I know this is what you're thinking, aside from the fact that those were your exact words on the day of the ride? I know because when I began loudly making fun of you for almost crashing out over a very minor shift in rider position, you turned around with flecks of saliva stuck to the corners of your mouth and shouted at the person behind you, "One more word out of you and...!" It's too bad that you didn't realize the obvious: Threatening us with "One more word!" was a guarantee that you'd get hundreds more words, none of them flattering.

In your eagerness to communicate how serious you were, you lost sight of what was happening in front of you (this can happen when you're looking backwards and foaming at the mouth in the middle of a tight, fast-moving pack), which caused you to veer again, wobble, and flail.

More friendly advice ensued. I think the dominant message was "Get away from that kooktard. What fucking kookfuck."

Where that puts us today

Unfortunately, on this, your second Donut Ride in the South Bay, you alienated at least as many people as you did on your first one. Remember last week? That was when you got into a screaming match with G3. Sadly for you, he videoed the whole thing with his GoPro. He comes across as reasonable. You come across as a dickhead with a Dallas-sized chip on your shoulder. That was also the same ride where your awful flailing bike weaves earned a reproof from another rider. You had the bad judgment to verbally accost him at the top of the climb, cementing your incipient reputation as a bona fide crazypants.

So after two group rides people are starting to say "Wow! Who is that kooktard?"

Others are saying "Wow! What a crazypants! Is that why they kicked him out of his own country?"

Still others are saying "Wow! For such an aggro attitude, he sure is weak on the bike. He got shelled like a bad pecan as soon as the pace got hard."

See?

No one is saying anything good about you. They are, to the contrary, saying bad things about you. This is not good for you or for them. Let me explain why.

No one cares who you are. They care how you are.

This bicycling thing we do is ostensibly for fun. It is also interdependent on the behavior of others. This means that bicycle riding makes us friends with people we would otherwise never associate with. Through bicycle riding I have become friends with some weird, strange, bizarre and fucked-up people, and even a handful of Republicans. Through bicycle riding I have learned that even though I may not see eye to eye with a person on every issue, when it comes to stuff like bike handling I had better swallow my pride and let guys like Dom and Walshy do their thing.

Neither was there today, but if they had been, and you'd showed them your impish attitude, the consequences would have been dire...for you.

You see, you are now riding among some people who have serious skills. Dom is just one of several bike wizards who can thread a needle at thirty-five through a wet, bumpy turn six inches off the wheel in front of him and never even think about tapping the brakes. That's very different from you, whose bike skills are more akin to mine: That is, they suck.

But back to the fun. It's fun to yell at people who do stupid, dangerous shit. There's the basic fun of just yelling at a kooktard crazypants, but there's also the fun of teaching. By pointing out your ridiculous moves we are helping you get better. This reduces the chance that we will get crashed out when you swerve twelve feet to avoid hitting a dead beetle.

However, it's not fun when the kooktard insists (is it okay if we call you KT for short?) that he was right and everyone else is the kooktard. It's not fun because our yelling is only fun when we do it once. When it escalates into screaming we go into oxygen debt and get dropped. It's also not fun because you are exhibiting the characteristics of someone who is not benefiting from our sage advice, and is, instead, doubling down on his kootardishness.

Why it all matters

The first reason is the simplest, KT. You are a buzzkill. Our happy feeling of "I'm riding my bicycle! Yippee!" dissipates for good when you imply that you will escalate the problem into a violent confrontation.

The second reason is because when you behave like a crazypants you will eventually feel terrible about it. Here's what happens: You begin by alienating lots of people. You keep riding with us. You get in a crash when you are hit by a car, kook out and clip a curb, run into someone while screaming at the person behind you, etc.

Then, because you're part of our community we stop to help you. We follow the ambulance to the hospital. We get your worthless ass checked in. We call your mother or mental healthcare specialist. We even bring you clean underwear; Tink can verify that part. We treat you with the same compassion and concern that we treat all our non-kooktard buddies.

Then, after they take the long plastic pipe out of your dick, staple your fucking head shut, and send you home with a suitcase of oxycodone (we drive you, by the way, you sorry shit), you realize that we're actually a pretty good bunch of bastards to have in your corner when shit goes sideways. Then you reflect about what a sorry ass kooktard crazypants you've been and you feel awful. You say something like "Guys, I don't know how to repay you," or "Let's put some shrimps on the barbie," or "New Zealand actually isn't anywhere near Canada and there's no bridge to Australia," but bottom line is you feel terrible.

Then, you feel worse because no one cares that you've been a dick. We were going to help you no matter how much of a kooktard you were. Even though you're a kooktard crazypants, you're our crazypants and we take care of our own, kind of like the village idiot who no one can make fun of except the villagers.

The third reason it matters is that you are a representative of your former penal colony. We often have awesome foreigners join our midst and they do much more than teach us how to speak proper English. Juliana, who is from Austria, a country similar to Australia, made everyone fall in love with her and not just because she was kind, warm, athletic, and smoking hot, although those things were all taken into due consideration.

We embraced her because she appeared to like us and to enjoy our company and she hammered it out on the NPR twice a week for an entire summer before going back to Sydney, the capital of Austria. We have a hard time thinking you like us, KT, when you behave like a crazypants.

In other words, you have a lot to share by teaching us about your great country. We would love to learn about it and watch you drink us all under the table like Alan, our favorite transplanted Welshman, who told us that the main difference between California and the UK is that in the UK "everyone is so grumpy." You're checking out on that score, by the way.

At bottom, we would love to learn about your culture and history and how your countrymen exercise such inhuman restraint when they're constantly surrounded by soft, fluffy sheep.

A word to the wise

I'm not sure exactly where you're from, but here in America we like to sue everybody. So when you escalate a verbal confrontation into a fistfight you can be assured that we will call the police. They will arrest you and the DA will likely file charges. You will spend $5,000 - $25,000 to get the charges dropped depending on whether it's a misdemeanor or a felony. Oh, and it's always possible you won't get the charges dropped. Imagine how embarrassing it will be when you return to your native land after ten years in

Corcoran State Prison with a tattoo on your butt made with a coathanger that says "Honey Hole."

And of course, if you really do beat up one of us spindly weak people, we will sue you in civil court for damages. You could lose everything you have, including your porn collection and all your Hello Kitty stickers. See? This just isn't worth it.

Kissing and making up

On the bright side, there's an easy way to fix all this. On your next group ride in the South Bay, approach one of the people you've been such a kooktard to and say "Hey, mate, I'm KT. Sorry for being such a crazypants."

They will say "No problem dude. It's just bicycling." Then we'll all go have a post-ride coffee and make fun of your dorky kit while secretly envying your cool accent.

Just as you've quickly earned a reputation for being a turd, people will start saying good things about you. They will respect you for admitting your kooktardishness and most importantly for erasing the buzzkill that now follows you around like a bad kimchi fart.

They will still yell at you when you kook out but you'll accept the criticism in the spirit it's intended, and after a couple more rides you'll feel like one of the gang.

See you soon, KT!

PS: The NPR leaves every Tuesday and

Thursday from the Manhattan Beach Pier at 6:40 AM. Please stop by to apologize, have your nose rubbed in a bit of poop, and enjoy some fun.

PPS: TELO crit race on Tuesdays at 6:00 PM, right around the corner from the Strand Brewery where, post-race, you can show us how they drink back in the Old Country.

IMPROVING YOUR
TECHNICAL SKILLS

"I'm really sorry, dude," the man said in an extremely apologetic and embarrassed tone of voice.

I looked at his sincere expression and was impressed by how badly he felt. He was a young fellow, nonplussed at the mix-up, and his first instinct was to do the right thing and apologize. I took all that into account and with a polite nod I accepted his words in the spirit they were offered.

Then I said, "Get off me you stupid fucktard," and pushed him backwards by the throat.

With the other hand I shoved and punched his chest, even as the cascade of idiots kept piling atop us, screaming, cursing, skidding, and clumping like a spaghetti bowl of arms, legs, helmets, bikes, cranks, chains, and wheels in a grimy sauce of skin, sweat, and sand.

First 'cross race ever.

First lap ever.

First technical spot on the course ever.

And mowed down from the rear like fresh meat in a men's prison.

I banged on the bars to straighten them, put the chain back on, got the brakes working, and hopped back on my bike. The last of the idiots from my sub-wanker Cat 4 "C" group had just started to scale the sand wall along the embankment at the end of the sand pit.

After a few pedal strokes I saw that the front derailleur no longer worked. At the bottom of the wall I dismounted and this occurred to me: "What kind of bike ride is it where you have to get off in a sand pit and scale a high wall made of loose sand?"

I struggled up the wall and this occurred to me: "What kind of bike ride is it where you have to carry your bike while running uphill in loose sand?"

I tried to remount, smashed my shin against the pedal and racked my nuts on the sharp end of the saddle. MMX had warned me against trying the jump-remount technique. This next thought occurred to me: "What kind of bike ride is it where you bloody your shins and bust your balls on the saddle?"

Then I tuned in to the fat bald guy at the top of the wall who was screaming so hard that his pale skull throbbed with swollen purple veins, "Puke and spit 'til you shit blood, goddammit! Puke and spit! Catch those bastards! Puke and spit!"

Next to him was an even crazier fellow who was profoundly drunk even though we'd yet to crack eleven o'clock. This gentleman had a giant black megaphone and it was stuck between his legs from the rear so that it looked like it was coming out of his ass. He had turned around so that the megaphone was facing the riders on the course, had bent forward and with his head between his knees and his lips around the megaphone he was mouthing farting sounds as loudly as he could.

This occurred to me: "What kind of bike ride is it where you're exhorted to puke and spit and shit blood and be faux farted on by drunks?"

The answer occurred to me in between rasping gasps and spurts of blood from my wounds: "It is cyclocross." And the race wasn't yet five minutes old.

Success in 'cross is one part preparation, nine parts Preparation H

I had arrived early and ridden two laps around the course. Set in the middle of a dustbowl in Costa Mesa that serves as a BMX track and breeding ground for thorns and snakes, the racecourse started with a few turns in hard-packed dirt and then went through a massive sandbox, up a wall, over a cement sidewalk lip that hit your rim so hard and so deep that your skull felt like it would rattle off your neckbone, through more dirt, up and over a tight mogul that accelerated into an off-camber mogul with a tiny chute off to the left that if you missed, it put you in the thorns and snakes but if you nailed it, it tried to throw you over the bars, then along more dirt to a jerk-up dirt mound also with a narrow chute that you could either nail and coast over or miss and stall out on the steep top of the mound, and then sharply down into a high-speed right with more thorns and loose sand, a brief respite of more dirt and dust along a flat section and then into the BMX bowl with a quick drop and climb, then down a head-first elevator drop, up along the edge, a 180-degree pivot and down a second elevator shaft, around a couple of turns and a fast drop followed by a straightaway until you hit the grass, which was hugely muddy, wending past trees that all shouted "Hit me!" and through more mud and around a turn and then what-the-crap-is-this-here where someone had placed a couple of barricades and you had to jump off and either time it perfectly or rack your shins and have the people behind run you over, and of course there were tons of people camped out next to the barricades to watch you trip and hopefully hang your bike on the lip of the barricade so that you'd bellyflop into the mud and then remount from a standstill if you'd garfed it up while the gazelles leaped back on their saddles without ever breaking stride or spearing themselves in the balls, through more grass and sharp turns and bingo — you'd have completed one whole lap and felt like you'd run a marathon with ankle weights, all the while people calling you a slacker and a sub-wanker and ringing cowbells and laughing and enjoying the comedy of watching you miserably ride your bike with a look of despair that said "I have only four or five thousand more laps to go."

Navigating the course seemed impossible at recon speed. Once the whistle blew it was ten times faster and a million times worse.

Taking Karma Bitch head-on

The race was as advertised: Sheer appendage-stomping agony at threshold with trees, barriers, sand, moguls, drop-offs, and briar patches at every turn. My swollen and bruised ankle banged against the crank arm every few pedal strokes until it was a bloody, throbbing mess of flesh and skin and blood ground into my pink unicorn socks. I chased and passed wanker after wanker, but never caught the leaders and never so much as caught sight of Crown Jules, who had done on the 'cross course what he did on the Donut Ride every Saturday: Show up, nod, and ride off from all the grown men.

After what seemed like days I saw Haunches on the sidelines and shouted out, "How many more laps?"

"This is it!" he said.

I sliced through a few more turns, crossed the finish line, and left the course filthy, bleeding, drained, sore, gasping, and, adding insult to injury, with a DNF because my ankle timer strap didn't work, meaning that my last or next-to-last placing never showed up on the sub-wanker Cat 4 result sheet which was posted, appropriately, on the back of the port-o-potties.

Five minutes later I stood on the start line for the 45+ A race, which was easily the second toughest field of the day, and which featured various hammerheads and a sprinkling of other veteran killers. MMX had summed it up when I told him I was doing the 45+ A's immediately after the sub-wanker race.

"Oh," he said. "So you'll be completely gassed before the race even starts."

MMX helped get my chain onto the big ring, as I'd ridden the previous race in the small one. The first-lap crash had broken my front derailleur. It's nice to start your race knowing you'll do the whole thing in the big ring. Having your fingers covered in a black, gooey tar made of grease and sand is an added bonus especially when you wipe your brow or your eyes.

The whistle blew and everyone rolled away. In the BMX bowl a kindly spectator shouted out, "Yo, Wanky! You're dead last! Do you hear me? DEAD FUCKING LAST! Get your ass up there and race your fucking bike!"

I had in fact heard, as the proximity of spectators to the edge of the course had allowed him to scream directly into my eardrum. So I hammered with my ears ringing loudly until I caught the one gasping, gaffed fish who was dangling ahead, passed him, and, no longer last, set the needle at "cruise" for the rest of the race. I got passed by the 35+ B racers. Then the 45+ B racers. Then a pack of kids. Then a flock of starlings. Then by an empty oil drum. And finally by Crown Jules. "What's he doing out here again?" I wondered. "He's already raced and won three times today. Isn't it his bedtime?"

When MMX and the leaders lapped me, I was

enjoying myself thoroughly. No longer compelled to dash crazily over the barriers, I daintily dismounted, stepped over each one, dusted the crud off my shoes, and remounted. No longer afraid of the sand pit, I coasted easily through it and walked — yes, walked — at a leisurely pace up the wall. Bald Dude and Farter looked on in disgust. "Aren't you even gonna try?" asked Bald Dude.

"Yep," I answered with a smile. "But not today."

IT DON'T MEAN A THING (IF IT AIN'T GOT THAT BLING)

I like to get places early. In fact, there's not really any such thing in my book as "too early," and this includes getting to bike races. However, like sharing a motel room, when you take up someone's offer of a carpool you have to go with the flow. And when the person offering the carpool is Roadchamp, you can forget toodling up to the event two hours beforehand in a compact and fuel efficient Prius.

You'll be arriving in the Bling Machine

The full-size Cadillac Escalade comes with diamond-encrusted, 18-inch alloy wheels, an adaptive suspension with electronically controlled shock absorbers that hold your balls when you drive, xenon headlamps, an auto-dimming driver-side mirror, a power liftgate for your 350-lb. spouse, rear parking sensors that make a cute "splat" noise when you flatten whatever's behind you, a triple-zone automatic climate control that lets you be freezing cold, steel-smelting hot, and perfectly cozy all at the same time, leather upholstery that's nicer than your living room couch, heated 14-way power front seats that are hot enough to blow dry your hair, heated second-row captain's chairs and a crisp set of officer's whites, power-adjustable pedals, remote start, an auto-dimming rearview mirror, Bluetooth hands-free cell phone connectivity so that you can drive without having to put your hands on the annoying steering wheel, OnStar to track your spouse's trysts, a Bose surround-sound audio system with a six-disc CD/DVD changer so that you'll finally have a use for that $15,000 collection of obsolete compact discs, and a navigation system with real-time traffic updates so that you'll know — surprise — that the 405 is at a standstill, and a built-in rear-view camera for close-ups of the outraged drivers you chop in traffic.

This is all standard, along with the recessed hidden pockets for caching dime bags and related drug paraphernalia.

But Roadchamp doesn't do "standard"

Why? Because "standard" is another word for "sucker." Step up to the luxury Escalade model and you get hardware upgrades including 22-inch chrome alloy wheels which are bigger and therefore better, a more sophisticated adaptive suspension (Magnetic Ride Control) so that you can rest even more comfortably when you fall asleep at the wheel, auto-dimming, high-beam headlights that can illuminate the high school football field in a pinch, and a sunroof — or rather, a moonroof — for when you cruise the 'hood making sure your girls are working.

Inside you'll find heated and ventilated front seats for ultra fast kimchi fart dispersion, directional fans that let you point the flatulence over to whichever passenger has earned your ire by suggesting you stop and ask for directions, a heated steering wheel that forever renders obsolete the need to warm your hands by sitting on them or sticking them in your gal's shorts, a power-release feature for the second-row seats that doubles as an eject button, and a blind-spot warning system for hitting blind people in just the right spot. The premium trim level adds power-retractable running boards for gang-banging on the fly and a rear-seat DVD video entertainment system with a ceiling-mounted screen so that your kids can watch the latest porn while you take them to their pole dancing lessons. Top-of-the-line platinum versions of this growling beast throw in all the bells and whistles including LED headlights, heated and cooled cupholders, and a DVD entertainment system with dual screens mounted in the front seat headrests.

People who still feel skimped even after deciding on this pimp model and want something more in terms of options and luxury typically decide to commute by yacht. These things, of course, are simply the creature comforts to make sure you hit the starting line well rested and spitting bling. To all the dopes shuttling their bike crap to the race in rusted out turdboxes that cost less than a good set of racing rims, eat your hearts out because there's one honking badass car bolted underneath this moving luxury hotel room, it's taking up a half-acre of parking spots, and it's not yours.

The SUV that gives Hummer fuel economy a good name

The obscene 6.2-liter V8 that puts out a sick 403 horsepower and 417 foot-pounds of torque with a six-speed automatic transmission and a manual-shift feature will ensure that you'll never get anywhere without gas stations evenly spaced at 300-yard intervals. The only downside to the power train is that the all-wheel-drive system lacks a low-range transfer case and features a default 40/60 front-to-rear power split that's mainly intended to provide added peace of mind when road conditions turn ugly. "Ugly" in this case doesn't mean four-wheeling like some low-rent plumber in a 4?4 Jeep. It means "ugly" as in having to run over smaller vehicles, pedestrians, cyclists, small trees, and anything else cluttering up your pavement or the sidewalk. When trying to speed away from the cops on a crack run, this baby will take a mere 7.5 seconds to go from zero to sixty, a relatively impressive number for a vehicle this size and for a car that, once it reaches sixty mph, can neither be steered without a rudder and mainsail nor stopped without a concrete blast wall.

New cylinder-deactivation technology that seamlessly shuts down and restarts half the engine's cylinders to save fuel is now standard, even though Escalade engineers snickered throughout the entire design process as EPA "estimates" stand at 14 mpg city/20 highway for the 2WD Escalade. This is a number which, if believed, makes you a potential investor in a Madoff fund which guarantees annual returns of at least 25%. Properly equipped, two-wheel-drive versions can tow a healthy 8,300 pounds or your mother-in-law, but not both.

Did these poor fellows take their Geritol?

We got to the race and it was pathetic. Since I'd revolutionized my training with the use of a power meter, doing build weeks that focused on intervals and endurance and including the appropriate amount of rest, it was foreordained that I was going to destroy the field. I felt sorry for the sods pedaling around the campground in a futile attempt to warm up.

In fact, I considered ditching the 45+ race completely and just doing the Pro/1/2 race. What kind of satisfaction would I get out of smacking the crap out of these old shoe liners? There was poor doddering Glass Hip, looking slower and weaker than a homeless man after a Chicago ice storm. There was ancient Herndy-Doo, at 6'4" and 185 lbs. Didn't he know he was way too big for a hard man's climbing race like Boulevard? Who was he kidding?

And of course I'd ridden up with Roadchamp, who, although admittedly on form, was going to get a big slice of manure pie shoved down his throat when I opened up the jets. Tired, sick, and mentally defeated DJ had emailed at the last minute to say he was going to race, so we'd gracefully allowed him to tag along. I spent my warm-up trying to pick just the right speech to deliver from atop the podium.

I was having difficulty deciding whether to begin with "And thou, vanquished warriors" or "Nice try, losers."

At the sign-in I calmly unrolled my training log and power meter data and showed it to the guy handing out race numbers. "See this, Freddie? You can just give me my medal and my money now and save these other fools the misery of having to get spit out the back."

He looked at me funny. "Who are you?"

"Wankmeister. Cat 3, 45+. You'll know my name after today, pal."

He rolled his eyes and gave me my number.

Lap One: Victory in the making

I made sure to start on the front row. Long experience had taught me that starting on the front of a long road race intimidates everyone, as there's nothing more demoralizing than seeing someone courageous and fit enough to elbow his way to the head of the field before the race even starts. I felt their mutterings of fear.

We rolled out and hit the first little wall. This was the place last year that had caused me so much difficulty a mere two minutes into the race. Now it was effortless, as if a pair of bionic legs had been bolted on at the hip. We crested the bump and began the rolling downhill that took about twenty-five minutes before you hit the first real climb of the day. Staying towards the sharp end but cannily out of the wind, I watched three no-hopers leap off the front. "Fodder for us hardmen who'll sweep them up like broken teeth after $1 shots in a Texas bar with fifty roughnecks and only one hooker," I thought.

Before long we crossed the railroad tracks and began the first climb. It took 5:25 and required 322w, and I made it over in fine form. After a brief respite we started the second section. The pace on this climb shelled twenty or more riders from the sixty-man field.

The second section of the climb took 6:47, killed off another clump of the feeble and the lame, and required 320w. However, halfway through the second section I noticed with some alarm an unpleasant burning sensation in both legs, a feeling that is often followed by getting dropped. Shortly after the feeling stabbed all the way up into my lungs, I found myself in a single file, desperately trying to hold onto the wheel in front of me. Still confident of the win, I nonetheless had to acknowledge that this degree of pain so early in the race was troubling, particularly since the rest of the field was chatting and stretching and eating and finally putting away the morning paper.

At forty-one minutes into the race we turned onto the big hill, a jagged 5.2-mile climb that reared up out of the earth like a tooth from the lower jaw of Charlie Sheen. At this moment Herndy-Doo attacked, smashing the group, shelling various hangers-on and forcing the remainder into a bitter single file. It took 706w to follow the attack, and 302w to make it to the top of the climb, although halfway up I got puked out the back with ten or fifteen others. Herndy's pace was so bitter that at the slight declivity midway through the climb the leaders sat up, frightened at what they'd unleashed. I and my group struggled back onto the lead pack, where I took a few moments to re-evaluate my victory speech. "It is with great honor that I accept these spoils of victory" or "I can't believe I beat you guys after that thrashing you gave me on the first lap." Either one would be appropriate.

Lap Two: It's not an endurance event until 90 minutes have elapsed

Everyone knew that my forte was endurance. This was really where I shined. So it was only a minor inconvenience that I got dropped and had to time-trail back onto the leading group. Once back with the peloton I was able to re-evaluate my competition. There was Richard the Unmeek, looking older than a bristlecone pine and clearly not up to the task at hand. There was Herndy, plainly cracked and hanging on for dear life after that pointless beating he had administered on the big climb. There was DJ, surviving, but just barely. There was Roadchamp, looking good but only because I had yet to unleash my Attack of Black Death.

There was only one rider in the field who was

up to the task at hand of winning, and that was me, because it's not an endurance event until you've been racing for ninety minutes. When I surveyed my victims I thought "This must have been how Genghis Khan felt when he looked down onto some modest city filled with plump victims and soft defenders who'd never faced the horse and the biting edge of the pitiless steel."

There was a 721w surge as we hit the bottom of the climb at the railroad tracks on the second lap. I found a good wheel. The next time I checked my watch we were ninety minutes into the race. "There it is! Get ready to hurt, suckas!"

We were almost a thousand feet from the summit of the climb, my GPS informed me after the fact. Roadchamp had been drilling it full bore for the last three minutes. I looked down to check my wattage when suddenly it broke. The "it" was me. In a few short seconds the pack had left me behind without even pausing to appreciate the intensity and fury of the Attack of Black Death I had been preparing to unleash. "Ungrateful bastards!" I cursed.

A minute later I crested the hill, put my head down, and time trailed up to the pack one more time. This time there would truly be no mercy as I shot to the front and put down the most fearsome and searing attack of the day. The entire field gasped in fear and exhaustion and pain, strung out in a wide group four abreast, sipping water and looking at their watches. I relented, satisfied that I'd made my point.

"Good pull," a passing rider said, trying to hide his fear with a friendly smile.

When we turned for the second time up the big hill, I decided that they'd had enough. "Why punish these idiots any further?" I said to myself. "I'm going to have to see them again next week so no need to rub their noses in it."

With that, I let them ride away, this time for good. I re-evaluated my podium speech for a third time. "I dedicate this DFL to my mother, my wife, and my children." Sounded pretty good to me.

The lead group became a tiny dot. Once they were out of sight I heard a noise like a sonic boom, later to learn that it was G$ who had attacked from the rear, catching the competition with their pants down, after which he had flown the coop for good. I was proud of him, as that was exactly what I had planned to do, only harder and faster. He time trailed the entire third lap, winning the race by more than two minutes.

Lap Three: This is how puppies feel when you rub their noses in it

Once I had magnanimously decided to let the others fight it out for the win — who cares about a stupid bike race anyway — the rest of the race was a blur. I ended up in a four-man wanker brigade: Larry from Coates Cyclery, who looked like he was a hundred but rode like a man twice his age; Moe from BL Bicycles, whose redeeming quality of being willing to pull endlessly was offset by his 4'11? frame that provided zero draft; and Curly from Bike Religion, who had found God and was force-feeding him to my soul via my aching, screaming, bleeding thighs. We traded pulls while battering each other like onion rings, miserably, senselessly, stupidly, and hopelessly until we crossed the tracks and began the final climb. We were broken old men clawing our way through the desert for the grand prize of not being DFL, and it would be a fight to the death.

My temporary teammates left me in the dust after the tracks and I dragged on, broken and alone, one mile from the Mexican border and almost desperate enough to take the next left which led into Mexico and try my luck with coyotes and drug smugglers rather than finish the race DFL. On the bright side, when you've been shelled and cracked and are straggling alone uphill to the finish line, you get to take note of the countryside and scenery. That's normally my favorite part of getting dropped, but this part of California is barren and ugly and studded with shrubby, spiny, desert vegetation. The sun here beat down hot and dry unless the wind happened to be blowing at thirty below, which it now was. I noted that the road color had gone from black to green, and pondered the road crew that had paved California's only vomitus highway.

"Say, Bill, pour me some more of that asphalt, willya?"

"Aw shit, Terrence, we're damn shore all outta

asphalt."

"Well hell we gotta pave it with something."

"My old lady's still sick in the back of the pickup from last night at the Golden Acorn."

"Let's just scoop up them puke baggies and dump it into the hot mix. Nobody'll ever know."

Midway through this reverie I passed a poor sap from the 35+ race who had started ahead of us. He was cramping and unable to pedal. There is nothing that gets me more motivated than someone going more slowly than I am except for someone who's hurting and wrecked from another race. "You okay?" I pretended to care.

"All cramped up," he moaned.

"You'll make it," I soothed him. "The finish is just another fifteen miles away, uphill with a headwind. But at least you're not stuck in freezing rain with hail like last year." He moaned some more and made as if to unclip and go lie down on a cactus.

"Take one of these," I said, and handed him a Hammer anti-cramp capsule that had been given to me before the race by a buddy. Just as he reached over, it slipped from my hand and I've never seen a cyclist intentionally lunge harder or faster for the pavement. He scooped it up and washed it down.

"You do massages?" he shouted as I dwindled in the distance.

Going for the glory

Imagine my shock when, a couple of miles

from the line, I was overtaken by a group of ten wankers from the 45+ field who were apparently even slower than I. In addition to ensuring that with a little strategy I wouldn't be DFL, I immediately saw that I could make an impressive showing in the final run to the line.

There is an unwritten rule in cycling that at the end of a race in which you are pack fodder it is unseemly to sprint. Team Wanker rolled by me, blathering loudly about their heroics during the first part of the race. They included three of the guys who had been in the no-hope breakaway that stayed out for well over a lap before splatting on the windshield of the hostile field. As we approached the line one of them turned to me, seeing me start to shift. "No, you don't," he warned.

A second wanker wheeled alongside. "We're not going to sprint for thirtieth are we? You're kidding me, right?"

All he got in response was my steely-eyed glint. Poor bastard didn't even know we were actually sprinting for 27th.

Easy as taking raw meat from the jaws of a pitbull, I unleashed the Sprint of Black Death and cruised over the line with bike lengths to spare. The spectators watched, slack-jawed that a racer with such speed and power was not racing with a squad from the Pro Tour. I heard them whisper as I roared by, "That's his first 27th placing of the year!"

My mission accomplished, I reviewed the

day's successes:

> 1. The only people who beat me were the ones who were faster, stronger, shrewder, and better at bike racing.

> 2. I got to save my victory address for the next week.

> 3. Roadchamp was still in the parking lot when I finished so I didn't have to walk the 180 miles back home.

> Just wait until next year.

LATIGO CANYON CLIMB

"How was the ride today, Dad?" my youngest asked when I wheeled in the bike after ninety-five miles up the coast, up Latigo Canyon, down Kanan Dume, down the coast, and back home up Via del Monte.

"It was fine," I said. Then I collapsed on the bed.

Mrs. Wankmeister hurried in. "Are you okay?" She was worried.

"Urgle," I answered.

So many things had happened on this glorious, sunny, eighty-degree day in Southern California that I couldn't begin to put them into a coherent whole, which made sense given the fact that I was incoherent for so much of the ride. What I could tell you though is this: There's something wrong with men who go in for bondage and whips and chains. The idea that some broad is going to put on a weird costume, tie you to a chair, and beat the crap out of your nether regions with a whip until you moan in pain, sob in agony, beg for mercy, and finally collapse in a wet puddle of self-loathing, blood, urine, and sweat, and that you're going to pay her for it ... that's sick.

It's sick because if you'd just shown up on the Saturday ride that morning you could have gotten all that and more for free.

Dame Vicious von Flogg

We began with a torrid pace at the bottom of Latigo, the vicious climb outside of Malibu that takes forty-five minutes if you're fast and much longer if you're not. Spider accelerated up the first little climb so I hopped on his wheel but was quickly shed. Checkerbutt and Fireman also got dropped, leaving me flailing off the back where I was quickly overhauled by Dame Vicious von Flogg, who weighs about forty pounds.

She cheerily hopped out of the saddle as she passed, tossing her rear wheel into my front fork. She had a bit of learning to do, but that's the peril of being a wheelsucker — you're at the mercy of the wheel you suck. The pain was almost unendurable as she gradually reeled in Fireman, who'd been dropped by Checkerbutt. "Yo, Fireman," I said. "You're getting caught and dropped by a chick!"

He fought viciously to get on my wheel, then took a hero's pull in the universal manspeak of "I ain't getting dropped by no chick." After that effort fizzled, Dame Vicious came back to the fore and laid down a relentless tattoo of kicks, punches, and blows to the groin. Before long Fireman began the Dangle of Death, opening gaps and then fighting to get back on. I was glued to von Flogg's wheel, eking out every tiny bit of draft from her tiny frame.

Dame Vicious then cheerily looked back.

"Goodynews!"

"Urg?" I asked.

"Yep! Daddy says I don't have to get a job next year and can spend another year getting in shape to ride my bike!"

"That sucks," I moaned, as Fireman hung his head, rolled his bloodshot eyes, and lolled his tongue in the Death Rattle of Drop.

Soon the road leveled into a milder incline, and von Flogg did the only sensible thing: She pulled out her riding crop, shifted into the big ring, and began to whale me about the head and shoulders, all the while chattily wondering what the best way was to learn not to throw her back wheel into my spokes as she threw her wheel back into my spokes. Every few minutes she'd pause the beating to let the accumulated blood drain from my eyes. We passed people like we were on a motorcycle. I greeted each one the same way: "You just got dropped by a chick."

Finally one of the droppees whom we passed said, "I am a chick!"

"That's even worse, then," I panted as Dame Vicious exchanged the whip for a chain that was studded with small sharpened spikes.

Soon we had Checkerbutt in our sights. Dame Vicious rode him down like a terrier overpowering a three-legged rat and as we passed him I said, "You just got hunted down and dropped by a chick."

"Well you've been sucking wheel the whole way, you wanker," he retorted. Then he added, in the universal manspeak of wounded ego, "I was taking it easy because I didn't want to be alone."

Suuuuuuuure you were.

Then he attacked us. I fought on and Dame Vicious countered, gapping Checkerbutt, who recovered and attacked again. By the fourth exchange I came unhitched, kind of like when a camper comes undone from a cheap U-Haul towing hitch midway up Loveland Pass. They exchanged blows all the way to the top, with Checkerbutt finally putting a three-second gap on Dame Vicious after a forty-minute full-gas climb.

Fireman caught me and flogged me and dropped me just before the summit. Spider was at the top enjoying his new sub-forty-minute conquest of Latigo. The rest of the wankers trickled in, each showcasing various stages of defeat, despair, and hopelessness.

Who were they, these feeble-legged bicyclists who couldn't keep up with Dame Vicious von Flogg?

Checkerbutt: Came up from the City of Cadmium and Mercury Poisoning to represent the Long Beach Freddies in a throwdown with the royalty of the South Bay. With the exception of Dame Vicious, who rode him down and made him sing for his supper, and except for the caning he got from Spider, he whipped the snot out of everyone else, ticking off a second place on Strava for the Kanan descent and giving me the leadout of all leadouts for the sprint at Temescal Canyon. I didn't have the heart to come around his sorry checkered butt, so I gave him a push as his innards began spilling out from his ears and gifted him the victory.

Tubetop: Sidekick to Checkerbutt, he rode the way we were more accustomed to seeing the Long Beach Freddies ride — weakly. This was his payback for the funny email he sent after the Solvang Century, in which he'd impugned the manhood of the strongmen of the South Bay. The last I heard from him was a distress phone call from Peet's in Santa Monica, asking Checkerbutt how to get back to his car in Manhattan Beach, twenty miles away.

DJ: Avoided the humiliation of having Dame Vicious von Flogg grind him under her jackboot by motoring on to Camarillo and opting out of the Latigo dominatrix chair.

Douggie: Coming back on PCH he unleashed the crusher attack of death on the short wall just before Latigo, decimating the already toasted group. Then he dropped himself, leaving me and Fireman to flog for a while until he and Checkerbutt caught back on. Despising the safety of Malibu Colony we opted for Pepperdine Hill. Fireman crunched it and Douggie followed through with the pull of black death, Checkerbutt gasping and me doing whatever happens when you breathe more deeply than a gasp. From that point on Douggie hammered like a madman. As we climbed onto Vista del Mar we got passed by an insane dude with one red pannier on a steel fixie, and he went by like we were standing still.

Unfortunately, that's when Douggie could actually smell the coffee at CotKU, and he ran down Mr. Fixie, who jumped in with me and Checkerbutt only to find that twenty-nine mph on a fixie means your legs come detached from your hips. I've never seen anyone sustain 350 rpm for a kilometer, but when his sacrum came tearing out his rectum it was all she wrote.

Knoll: Had the misfortune to popularize the ride as "mellow"' when in fact it wound up being Sledgehammer of the Broken Lower Spine. Knoll utilized every trick in the book but came up a few chapters short, at least by his usual standards, i.e., pummeling the snot out of me on long climbs.

Hockeystick: Took one brief pull on PCH, failed to alert the peloton to parked cars, to overtaken Team in Training-ers, to crevasses in the road, etc. However, eyeing the Belgian Waffle Ride on offer the following weekend, he opted for an even longer route with more climbing after Latigo.

Jens: The man who least deserved to be nicknamed after Jens Voigt lived up, yet again, to his reputation as Go to the Front Antimatter, a unique force in the cosmos that is diametrically opposed to ever taking a pull. However, he momentarily overcame this powerful negative attraction to sharing the work when he was observed engaging in a micropull on PCH for .000093 seconds, measuring a power output of 12 watts. Progress!

Arkansas Traveler: With the absence of Nancy,

Arkansas Traveler took up his rightful place at the back of the peloton ascending Latigo. When I descended to see if he'd been killed and eaten by a mountain lion, I found him doing with Junkyard what he'd done the week before with me — enjoying the ride. What's with that guy? Or should I say, "Respect."

Toronto: No matter how many megadeals he crafts during the week, nothing, and I mean nothing, can ever stop Toronto from joining the mob and taking his beating like a man. Always in line to take his pull (though usually melting away just as it's his turn), always ready to crack and flail when the riding crop falls about his tender parts, Toronto got his revenge on Dame Vicious von Flogg atop Latigo by unzipping his jersey and grabbing hold of his paunch to show us the source of his climbing non-prowess. This led to a paunch-off, where each of the weak, flaccid, elderly, and thoroughly beaten old men took turns comparing the amount of flab they could grip in one fist. Dame Vicious staggered over to the side of the road and vomited, and justice was done.

Skinbag the Advice Sausage: On the way back, Skinbag advised me that although Dame Vicious had dropped every single man except for Checkerbutt and Spider, he'd put the wood to her on the Kanan descent. I corrected his deluded version of events. "Dude, she waited for half an hour at the top of Latigo for your sorry ass. If it'd been a race she'd have gotten to the bottom of Kanan with enough time for a pedicure before you showed up."

"Well, she's riding illegally."

"Illegally?"

"Yes. Those aren't junior gears."

"Dude, she's twenty-two."

THE BELGIAN WAFFLE RIDE, OR, FEAR AND LOATHING IN NORTH COUNTY SAN DIEGO

When our small pack of starving, thirst-ravaged, beaten down wankers hit the second rest stop at Mile 65.4, it was pandemonium. Fistwads of BonkBreakers, heads doused in cold Coke, unpeeled bananas devoured whole, and all the while smokin' hot SPY babes making hashmark soup of our numbers to ensure we were credited for reaching the checkpoint, and me racing straight for the water, refilling my bottle, and jumping back aboard my bike while most of the others were still gobbling PowerBars, sticking a finger down their shorts to see how egregiously their stinky diapers needed changing, or just rolling in the dirt and softly moaning.

    A hundred yards past the transfusion station it hit me. Whenever your ride involves a half-naked woman in her eighties wielding a broom and threatening to kill you with it, you've just crossed the threshold from epic and wandered over into the batshit crazy realm of the surreal. In fact, my last encounter with a crazy octogenarian woman during a bike ride didn't involve one who was half-naked or carrying a broom, it involved one who was completely naked and barefoot and ten miles from the nearest farmhouse.

Spanky Muffins

Spanky Muffins, or Clanghorn Leghorn as he was also known, had been whooping it up on the side with a cute little package from Granger, the only town in Texas that still had a Czech newspaper, and as far as I know, the only one that ever did, or for that matter, that ever had a Texan of Czech descent who could read.

I don't remember her name because I always called her Czechmate, and that particular morning in July of 1984 as I rolled up the frontage road along I-35 to pick up Spanky Muffins at his house for a ride, I could tell from a distance something was amiss. For one, in front of his little white rental shack there was a silver Z-car, and the only person I knew who drove a silver Z-car was his fiancee, the little ballerina who I always called "Bally."

For another, from the distance and angle I could see a maroon Ford pickup parked out on the back lot, partially obscured by the mesquite and the brokedown storage shed. Clanghorn didn't own a car and the only person I knew with a maroon pickup was Czechmate.

For yet another, I could see the side window that abutted Spanky Muffins's bedroom, and it looked like a head was sticking out, a head with long brown hair, which was odd because Spanky had a crew cut. Even from that distance I could hear the godawful pounding on his screen door and see a highly agitated Bally making more racket than a ninety pound ballerina ought to be able to make.

The only reason I knew we weren't going to need a homicide detective was because Bally had approached from the north and thus couldn't see the truck out behind the house, and also because on most days Bally didn't carry a handgun.

By the time I got up to the fence Spanky was slowly opening the front screen door in tandem with Czechmate falling clumsily out of the back window in her panties and hopping like a crazy woman through the goatheads and fire ant mounds to the safety of the thorny mesquite and her pickup, where she, unlike Bally, carried a handgun every single day of the year. Bally jumped inside the house and was yelling so loud that she never heard Czechmate drive away. I played dumb, wandered into his bedroom while they screamed, and did a disappearing act with Czechmate's clothes and shoes that would have made Houdini blush.

No country for old women

Spanky finally convinced Bally that nothing was amiss, and she was never the wiser until the big shindig the night before their wedding when I drunkenly raised my glass and made a toast that unfortunately wandered off onto the topic of

Czechmate and how glad I had been that Bally had left her .45 at home that morning. That, along with their subsequent divorce after the world's shortest marriage, is another story.

This story is about how Spanky and I decided that Bally was going to be laying in wait for him most of the rest of the day, so the only way to throw her off the scent was to go do a nice long 120-miler. The only problem was that it was now 8:00 AM and the temperature had already hit 104 and if we waited much longer it was going to get hot. Spanky thought he knew a couple of routes that would at least take us near a convenience store where we could get water, so off we went. By mile ninety we were delirious. The temperature was well over 110 and the ambient air temperature a few feet off the asphalt was easily 130. He got turned around and we missed the convenience store so we now had to either get something to drink or die.

By some miracle we hit a low-water crossing that was mostly filled with nasty green stuff from a dairy farm upstream but we were pretty sure we didn't have to worry about brain damage, as no one would notice, and we did have to worry about dying of thirst, so we filled our bellies and bottles on that nasty green sludge, which was the sweetest and best tasting water I've ever had in my life, notwithstanding the cramps that night followed by the vomiting and diarrhea that ensued for the next three weeks.

As we rode out of the shade from the water

crossing, ten miles from the nearest farmhouse, we saw a figure approaching us in the distance. As we got closer we saw it was a woman. A very, very old woman. Naked. Barefoot. Walking on that frying pan asphalt looking as starry-eyed batshit crazy as we felt.

At first neither of us could believe it. "You see that?" I asked Spanky.

"Uh-huh."

We pedaled slowly by. "Hi, ma'am," I said.

She never looked to the right or the left, and I couldn't help noticing that her body was perfectly brown all over with nary a tan line anywhere. "Hey," Spanky said after we passed.

"Yeah?"

"Why don't we just pretend that never happened?"

"Deal."

No country for lycra-clad wankers on the BWR

Back to 2012 and the inaugural Belgian Waffle Ride, while I'd been downing plasma and EPO tabs at the transfusion station, a group of twenty riders had taken a hard right turn down the dirt road that led to the quagmire of mud and water and slop and hell known by the bitterly ironic name of Country Club Road. As I made a right turn in their wake I was surprised to see them all coming back again, pedaling pell-mell and screaming at the top of their lungs: "Turn back! There's a crazy lady with no teeth and a broom barring the way!"

All the motivation I needed to go full steam ahead was the chance for an encounter with a crazy, toothless Broom Hilda. On I went until there in the distance I could see her hopping up and down in a blue fury, one-piece burlap sack jostling about her skinny frame, three-foot breasts slinging thisaway and that like two bad dancers, one of whom wants to tango and the other of whom wants to do crossword puzzles.

"No blog," I thought as I got closer, "will ever top this." Then, as I saw her making some pretty fair batting cage slices with the broom, cuts that, if they connected, would at least be good for a ground rule double, it hit me: Crazy half-naked lady with three-foot breasts doing major league swings with a broom can only mean that her son, who is probably also her husband and the father of her grandchildren, has finally pulled on his burlap bag, loaded the guns, and drained the rest of the turpentine bottle prior to going out on the porch to see which raccoon or possum or skunk or crow or lizard or trespasser he's going to have to shoot the legs off of.

"Fuck the blog," I thought. "I'm outta here."

The surrealistic hell of the North County

After a mad dash I connected with the pack that had flown from Broom Hilda, a completely different amalgamation of riders than the dead and dying who I'd left at the doping station. The inaugural Belgian Waffle Ride was already an unmitigated nightmare of brutish proportions. It had begun with the awful premise that 120 miles and 10,000 feet of climbing would kill most of the participants. The last thing I could clearly remember was the sight of MMX churning away at the front on Green Canyon Road, grinding up each roller with the nasty efficiency of an industrial food processor.

As I had struggled at the back, bladder almost bursting, I could only think with bitter fondness about the pee stop at mile twenty. We had all dismounted except for MMX, who had urinated while riding his bike, splashing a fine, twelve foot film of hot piss along the public bike path and most of his hand. "Why can't I do that?" I wondered. Several miles later, when I watched him absentmindedly wipe his nose and mouth, I wasn't quite as envious.

By Mile 39 the lead group had less than fifty riders, many of whom were already gassed from the high speed run-up to the first sprint followed by the inhuman attack up the mile-long gravel road that looked like it had been paved with artillery shells. The schmoes who had showed up uninvited to bandit the ride had long ago been crushed and shat out the back, and those who had shown up with minimal preparation were already well into the most miserable day of their lives, a day more awful than the first time they rode an aluminum road bike or wore a yellow Livestrong bracelet.

During the neutral portion of the ride I had found myself next to a giant dude in a purple jersey.

"Name's Fred," he said with a perfectly straight face. "I'm a track racer from back in the day. Mounting my comeback."

I looked at him to see if this was part of an elaborate joke. It was and it wasn't. "I don't think there's a velodrome on the route today," I offered.

"Yeah," he muttered. I never saw him again.

The crazies come out when it's muddy

My next companion was Singlespeed Nutter, the guy who would have won the psychedelic batshit crazy jersey if one had been on offer. In preparation for the 120-mile deathfest, he had shown up with his hairiest legs and his best single-speed bicycle. "I'm a 'cross dude, dude," he said.

"Really?" I thought. "I mistook you for a kooktard." He turned out to be very much the badass, as I would find out about seventy miles later.

But the most amazing person of all was the rider from Los Angeles who showed up to bandit the ride and shamelessly helped himself to all the goodies. He too was quickly shed.

Not too far into the ride my legs began burning as I hung on the back and I realized that I could either force myself to hang for another fifteen or twenty miles and then be completely wrecked or I could drop off the back and pee so that my bladder didn't rupture. It's amazing how easy a hard ride becomes when you get off your bike.

After remounting I settled into my own pace,

and the remnant grupettos from the wanker rear guard began to pass me, first in ones and twos and then in small groups. Like the old sailor in "The Rime of the Ancient Mariner" I tried to warn them of what awaited.

"Yo, Swami's dork! Have you done this course before?"

"Nah. Why?"

"Because you're going too hard. You will implode at Mile 80 or before and will have to cut the course and thereby cheat in order to finish. Ease up now while you're still behind."

They nodded and zoomed off. I saw them all again, of course, many miles later in varying states of collapse and disarray.

The end of reality bleeds over into the impossible and false

Keeping a steady pace I hit the bottom of Couser Canyon, and three quarters of the way up the climb I realized that my bottles were empty. With less than a quarter mile to the top I spied a blue support pickup parked on the side of the road. "Got any water?" I called out.

"Sure do!"

I hesitated because I was carrying my own very expensive bottles. I didn't want to give them up but I didn't want to carry them empty and I didn't want to collapse from heat prostration. As I slowly rolled by I reluctantly handed the guy my bottle. He thrust the replacement in my hand. It was icy cold. I glanced at it. Same as mine.

Before I could fling my bottle away like some talisman from the Twilight Zone, the two dudes were giving me a mighty push to restart me on the climb. The water was life giving. The bottle was brand fucking new. I never saw them again.

Fast forwarding past the Broom Hilda turn, the grupetto turned left onto a dirt road at Mile 66. With the exception of the lead group and a few other individuals, most of the Belgian Waffle Ride victims missed this turn. They were easy to spot because their bikes, legs, and shoes were devoid of thickly caked mud and slime at ride's end, and because the first words out of their mouths on completion weren't "Oh my fucking Dog, that dirt road with the 18% sandy wall and the narrow, deep river crossing with a rock ledge drop off and trench mud embankment on the other side followed by two miles of the nastiest, bitterest, slidingest, badassedest unpaved mud pit known to man was AWESOME!!!"

Instead, they would say in a noncommital sort of way, "Oh, yeah...I, uh, did that section. It was the wide water thingy, huh?" or "I dunno I just followed everyone else."

I just followed everyone else

Problem is, everyone I was following made the turn. We launched down the mud to the rock ledge and mayhem ensued. People slid to a halt, fell off their bikes, toppled over, yelled, cursed, and rode exactly like you'd expect roadies to behave when greeted by wet mud.

Singlespeed Nutter and another insane person flung themselves into the water as if death and maiming were something destined for others and not them, hammered up the other side, and quickly gapped everyone else by a hundred yards. The rest of the herd quaked and slipped and flopped over into the mud. As I hurtled down the embankment, unable to see the water, I only thought one thing, back from the day that Fields tried make me a 'crosser going around the golf course off of Red River street in Austin, and me trembling every pedal stroke of the way: "Just go fast!"

Fast I therefore went. So fast, in fact, that the only thing I heard when I launched into the river was "Holy fuck!" from some wanker who was lying in the mud and whose head I almost took off with my rear wheel. I landed full force on my front wheel in the water, and to my amazement the bike of its own accord rocketed up the other side. Speed was in fact my friend, although the guy lying in the mud with the broken frame, leg cut open to the bone, and tire tracks across his back wouldn't have agreed as he'd hit the crossing at full speed, but then again — and all this flashed through my mind in an instant — maybe his full speed just wasn't fast enough. My bike bounded up the embankment and went faster.

There aren't many times in your life when everything around you stops except you as if you were in a Nike commercial or a Spider Man slo-mo special effect movie scene. It happened that day. The riders up ahead froze and became part of the canvas. I followed their perfect line and as my bike jumped and jolted up behind them I muttered, "Coming through!"

Purple Jersey Andy heard something fearsome and looked back in terror. "Holy shit!" he yelled "That's his breathing!"

The noise coming from my lungs was so deep, so racking, so nasty, so fraught with spit and snot and spray and flecks of flesh that I fully expected to have to get off and poke my lungs back down my throat with a stick. But I didn't. Riders 1 and 2 vanished in my rear view, or would have if I'd had one. I hit the sand wall that made up the next insurmountable obstacle and went harder. Before I could vomit, the entire section was over and the crippled, broken remnants that were still wiping the mud off their asses might as well have been in Waco.

It's the only badass thing I have ever done on a bike. It's certainly the only badass thing I did on the BWR, because the rest of it was a nasty slog to the finish, overtaking one shattered rider after another until I hooked up with Mad Stan and Daffy Dave from the Wolfpack. They worked me over for miles, their shiny bikes proof that they'd avoided the muddy test of mettle, and despite shellacking them on Questhaven, they rode me down after Double Peak and we finished with A Day in the Life of Ivan Stefanovich, the long-haired Swami's dude who had knocked over twelve bikes and three helpers at the last feed station as he fought off the L.A. Bandit Cheapass Fuckstick for the last swig of Coke and the last fistful of pretzels. He had passed me on Double Peak like a man on a mission.

Only the strong survived

The BWR got its inspiration from Dave Jaeger and his annual French Toast Ride, a 118-mile death march held every January as a tune-up for the first road race of the season, the Boulevard RR. No one in the SoCal peloton exemplified the qualities of toughness, fairness, good humor, and great perspective as well as Dave. So it was fitting that when the race leaders wandered off course and failed to complete the entire route, it left Jaeger to claim the winner's jersey.

The color purple

The Belgian Waffle Ride started with a basic tenet: There will be winners, losers, finishers, and non-finishers, and they will be determined by relying on each rider's honesty, sportsmanship, and personal integrity. After the laughter subsided at the ridiculous notion that a bunch of scuzzball cyclists would do anything other than lie, cheat, and steal when swag was at stake, it was re-emphasized at the start line that the concept of "It's okay to cheat" doesn't apply. This was of course ignored, but to punish those who flouted the rules of fair play, at the end of the day the biggest cheater would be awarded a purple jersey.

The Belgian Waffle Ride was also unique because on the one hand it was billed as a true hardman event, but on the other it counted Top Dog as a participant. Those who had ridden with this softman of cycling knew that despite having been banished from California and sent to live in Kansas, no cycling event existed at which Top Dog could not garner the lion's share of the attention. Worse, his time spent trawling the barren cornfields and meth shacks in and around Lawrence mean that when he showed up he was in particularly fine form.

Whether by chasing down beginning cyclists and berating them for their choice of bicycle, the color of their jersey, or their pretensions to athleticism by daring to be ahead of him, or whether by instigating confrontations with violent motorists and then leaving the mayhem for others to deal with, or by simply whining about his back surgery/broken teeth/brain replacement therapy/AARP membership status as the reason he flailed and got dropped, when Top Dog rode, people took notice.

The BWR was no different. In an event designed to rely on the integrity of the participants, Top Dog floated to the surface of the tank like the very biggest and smelliest chunk, while the participants could only stare in shock like a hapless economy class passenger stuck next to the toilet door on a fifteen-hour flight to India. Some observers noted that Top Dog had been strangely absent along the muddy road of death. Others remarked that although he rode manfully through the water after the third water crossing, he fell into the mud after crossing it in the manner of a complete dirt noob, resulting in a boo-boo to his knee, which he later pointed to as proof of his toughness under fire.

While wildly claiming to have completed the course ahead of his betters as he swooped in to snare his finisher's tee-shirt, his finisher's bottle of commemorative ale, and his finisher's BWR jersey, Top Dog failed to produce his number with the proper hash marks proving he'd passed through all the check stations, and, what was worse, he claimed to have conquered Double Peak when he was seen sneaking past the turnoff to this bitterest of climbs while glued to the wheel of...oh shame!...a triathlete. In a later document entitled, "Affidavit and Declaration under Penalty of Perjury Regarding the Performance of Top Dog on the Belgian Waffle Ride," he was even audacious enough to claim that after slinking away from the finish area before being awarded the ignominious purple jersey in absentia, he had gone off in search of Double Peak in order to find it and climb it once he learned that he'd "missed it by mistake."

Unfortunately, Top Dog was unable to locate this mysterious hidden landmark, as it's only the highest point in San Diego County and looms 1,666 feet over the city of Carlsbad like a single rotten tooth jutting out from the sunken gum off an ogre. Plus, he had to hurry back to Kansas in order to spend time with his family.

As a result, Top Dog received the dreaded purple jersey, an item of clothing reserved for the lamest rider of the entire BWR. On the plus side, it came with a matching pair of purple sunglasses. If you ever want to see the whole ensemble in action, though, you'll have to head out to the byways of America's desert meth labs, as rumor has it that Purple Jersey Top Dog will not be invited back.

So how hard was it, really?

My secret to finishing this grueling course turned out to be simple: Eat lots of cheeseburgers and fries the day before, and realize that I was a wanker amongst men with no hope of following the leaders, and ride accordingly by never going into the red. Towards the end, after the last heart and lung transplant station, I fell in with a guy named Scott who had the ugliest jersey in the peloton. We stayed together through Bandy Canyon and Via Rancho, the place of my spiritual death, and through most of Elfin Canyon. More than the difficulty, this ride was memorable for its striking natural beauty, for its snow-encrusted mountain peaks, for its leafy green Spring foliage, for its streams, its chiseled rock faces, its piercing blue sky, and most of all for the mob at the last aid station that frantically fought for food as their last ebb of strength and morale failed them before the longest, hardest, most brutal and unforgiving part of the ride was to pitilessly crush them into broken and whimpering fools.

To SPY Optic and the people who made this great event happen, including the wearers of the yellow jersey (overall winner), green jersey (sprint winner), blue jersey (hardman), polkawaffle (KOM), and hideous purple jersey, I eventually said thank you once the tubes had been removed and I was well enough to get out of bed.

TOUR DE SHITSTORM

"I've got a spare seat on my plane if you'd like to join me for the Tour de Palm Springs Century this weekend," read Wehrlissimo's email.

"Fuckin'-A!" I replied, still not sure even after all these years what the difference was between, say, fuckin-A and fuckin-B, or fuckin-C for that matter. The chance to do a century ride after my recent beatdowns at Boulevard Road Race and the Red Trolley Crit would be a significant ego-building opportunity where I could whizz by lumbering freddies and feel fast, superior, and successful. No matter that "I won the century ride" has all the street cred of "I got laid by my wife."

The last time I had flown a private plane was when I did the hop from Geraldton, in West Australia, over to the Abrolhos Islands to see a colony of Brown Noddies and to get a picture of a nesting Red-tailed Tropicbird. It was a two-seater crop duster with pontoons. The pilot was eighty years old and coughed the entire way like he was going to die as he smoked no-filters and spit bloody phlegm out the window. The noise had been deafening and the water landing horrible beyond belief. I hoped Wehrlissimo's rig would be an upgrade.

I, Triple, Polly, DJ, and Wehrlissimo stood on

the tarmac of the Hawthorne Airport in the dark as Captain Doolittle loaded our bikes into the King Air Turboprop. Wehrlissimo had bought the entire airport, one of the largest in Los Angeles County, at a foreclosure sale. I hoped the same wasn't true for the turboprop.

This was traveling in style. Rather than driving across the desert for two hours and then fighting for five hours through L.A. traffic to get home we'd be landing in Palm Springs in thirty minutes and home by three in the afternoon. I reminded myself of all these advantages when Doolittle turned to us and said, "We're going to have to dip down aggressively once we cross the mountains in order to hit the landing strip, as it's just on the other side. There might be some turbulence."

"Dip down aggressively?" I wondered. "What the hell does that mean?"

A few moments later I found out because the airplane pointed straight down. We could see the approaching ground through the windshield and the only thing missing was a gun sight through which we could have strafed the airport. "Just like a roller coaster," I thought. "With no rails."

I glanced over at Triple. His thighs were held tightly together as if he were trying to keep something unpleasant from sneaking out of his butthole. Then we hit "some turbulence." The entire aircraft shuddered as if it had been smacked with a giant club. We plunged, hit another air pocket, shuddered again, and a warning light went off with a shrill beep. This was the part in a disaster movie when the captain comes on the intercom and says, "Please place the plastic cup over your mouth, tighten the strings with one hand, and with the other wipe up your bloody stool."

I looked at Polly, whose teeth were clenched, not even pretending to be cool. DJ had been okay until his engineer's hearing had picked up the sound of the warning beep as the plane's avionics alerted the entire cabin to the fact that we were about to die. Now he looked scared, too. I took a final glance at Triple and could only think, "I'm glad I'm not the chamois in his shorts."

Fortunately, Cap'n Doolittle got us onto the tarmac and Triple got quickly into the airport restroom for a thorough wipedown and a clean pair of shorts.

Welcome to Hell

The game plan had been to hook up with Uberfred and his Long Beach Freddies, administer a thorough South Bay beatdown to our rivals across the way, grab lunch, and jet back home while the boys from Cadmium Bay toiled away in the traffic like the irradiated slugs they were. After making the obligatory jokes about Long Beach's air pollution, terrible water, and mercury contamination, we learned that Uberfred had not planned on being anyone's victim.

The moment our combined group of twenty-six hit the edge of town, it became clear why the city of Palm Springs was developed as one of the first wind farms in California. Wind turbines require winds of up to thirty-five miles per hour in order to achieve optimum efficiency. As we followed the route along North Indian Canyon Road, which left the city and exposed us to the full crosswind that was powering the wind farm's "optimum efficiency," mayhem ensued because what was maximally efficient for the wind turbines was flat fucking catastrophic for the chubby little bicycle riders out for a pedal in the desert.

We'd started about 7:30 AM and the road was clotted with thousands of freddies on bicycles who had begun an hour earlier. The thirty mph crosswind was blowing people completely off the road. Every couple of hundred yards there were bicycles lying in a huge tangle, with hapless freddies trying to dislodge their $5,000 bikes from what was now part of a giant bicycle parts bazaar.

Uberfred gassed it and we clawed onto his wheel as we zoomed by the endless line of flailing riders. Since the crosswind was so strong, we had to echelon across the entire road. This meant that each time we passed a clump of struggling wankers, Uberfred would roar, "Riders!" but the freddies wouldn't hear until we were right on their asses. Many of them, cleverly riding deep dish wheels, would jerk to the right, the wind would catch their wheels, and they'd go sailing off the road and into the thorn-filled sand-and-gravel ditch, presumably to be eaten by snakes or stabbed to death or blinded by the six-inch cactus spines.

By mile three there were long lines of riders who'd simply given up, turned around, and headed back to Palm Springs. For us, there would be no quitting, as the Long Beach Freddies' favorite insult was to shout "You're weak!" whenever someone quit, got dropped, got passed, turned around, swung off the front, took a drink, stopped to pee, sucked his thumb, or cried for his mommy.

A confederacy of dunces

The whole idea of having twelve thousand idiots on bicycles in a venue designated as "ideal for a wind farm" did not happen by coincidence. It took the conspiracy of core stakeholders to come up with something this awful.

President of the local hospital: "Let's do something that will fill the beds! February's a slow month; we won't really be rocking until all of the drug overdoses at Coachella in April."

Coalition of local bike shops: "Let's do something that will require thousands of people to come to our town and completely replace their bikes."

President of the Chamber of Commerce: "We can showcase the beauty of the desert by routing the ride through all 427 stoplights and through each of the nineteen bedroom communities, all of which look alike."

Bill Snooker, Owner of Bill & Snooker Used Auto Emporium: "Make sure the route takes 'em by each of my fourteen lots. Never know when some idiot'll throw in the towel and want to drive home."

Crazy Sam Throckmorton, Desert Survival Adventures, Inc.: "Put twelve thousand city slickers on bikes on pothole-filled, thorn-littered, gravel-and-glass-and-nail-strewn desert roadways a thousand miles from nowhere, watch 'em flat and wander off into the scrub and ocotillo looking for water, then do emergency rescues and charge $859 a head to bring 'em back alive. Works ever' time!"

Freddy Freeloader, 2012 president-elect, Palm Springs Friendly Riders' Club: "It'll be just like the Solvang Century Ride! That's one of the most popular rides in America!"

It really wasn't anything at all like Solvang

After five miles of battering along in a full echelon as the howling crosswind sprayed curtains of sand and grit into our eyes and noses and teeth and buttholes, with freddies flying off the road and smashing into each other, and with Uberfred and DJ drilling the pace the whole way, we turned left directly into the wind. Never in my life have I been so happy to have a headwind. For one, it meant no more leaning at a thirty-degree angle to keep from being blown over. For another, it meant true shelter, not the misery of the partial draft you get from an echelon.

This respite only lasted a couple of miles

before we turned back into the crosswind. Uberfred hit the gas again, exploding the remnants of his flailing Long Beach soulmates. I hadn't bothered to look at the course map and had no idea how long this hell was going to last. For all I knew, it would be fifty miles out into the sandstorm and fifty miles back. My resolve began to fade and defeatism set in as the line of quitters and the clumps of the crashed flashed by.

After two more miles of crosswind hell, the road turned into tailwind heaven. I couldn't believe it. Uberfred, after flagellating us mercilessly for the first twelve miles, held up his hand. "Let's regroup!" he said.

I looked at DJ. He looked at me. We both thought the same thing, knowing that "regroup" was Uberfred-speak for "I need a pee stop and some rest and a nap."

"He's weak," said DJ as he dropped his chain down a cog.

I love you, that's why I hate you

The next sixty miles went by quickly, you know, where "quick" means "sitting in the dentist's chair getting a laparoscopy without anesthetic," a combination of straight tailwind and tail-crosswind. Uberfred would hammer until he'd dropped all of his friends, and then make us stop so that they could all catch up and he could catch his breath. Wash, rinse, repeat. By mile seventy we were well into the bowels of the poorly marked, suburban, stoplight-filled portion of the course.

At the final rest stop one of the Long Beach Freddies regaled me with the tale of a heart attack he'd had while cycling a few months back. "Yeah, I was with the guys and just keeled over."

"What happened?" I asked.

"Piece of plaque came off an arterial wall and chugged into my heart. Everybody has plaque on their arteries. Mine just lodged in a bad place."

"Yeah, right," I said, eyeing his enormous beer belly. "Is that what the doctor said?"

"Yeah. He said everybody has it."

"Did he graduate from a medical school in the Caribbean by any chance? Last name Sojka?"

Freddie looked at me funny. "No. But the good thing about it was that the guys were there for me."

"Really?"

"Yeah. They waited until I'd stabilized in the ICU before they all came in and told me I was weak."

"Well, at least you're back on the bike," I said, trying to make a positive out of a quadruple negative.

"I took a long time off the bike to recover, it being a heart attack and me almost dying and everything."

"How long were you off?"

"Four weeks."

Realizing that I was dealing with a madman, I got back on the bike and continued pedaling.

Anybody can pedal a bike seventy miles...

"But can they drill it for the last thirty?" That was DJ's question, and Uberfred answered it with a simple question phrased as a whimper.

"Hey guys," he said. "Let's just ride steady two by two for the rest of the way. Okay? Okay?"

DJ correctly saw that Uberfred was about to implode and was trying to entice him to slow down. DJ smiled a nasty smile, then went to the front and set a pace to match his smile. Sammy Poseur sidled up alongside him to match the pull, but after a couple of minutes he went rocketing off to the side in the rickety wobble of someone who is blown and not coming back.

I came to the fore and was joined by Large Arms. He had done the entire ride in booties, a skinsuit, and full TT rig which included fancy tri-dork water bottles attached to his saddle. However, his thrashing hams and swollen buttocks jiggled with such ferocity that they caused his forty-dollar insulated water bottles to fly out of the holders and into the spokes of whomever was on his wheel. Showing the most grit of all the freddies with the exception of Heart Attack, who we fully expected to die at any moment, Large Arms matched the pace for a solid five miles.

Ultimately his head drooped, his fanny pooped, and he did the wobble-and-fade to the ignominy of the rear, wheelsucking as best he could with Uberfred and what was left of the Cadmium Crew. With eighteen miles to go, DJ came up and joined me. It was as nasty and unpleasant a finish as I can recall, with countless stoplights and so many wrong turns that we eventually gave up on finding the course and pounded back to Palm Springs on the truck-filled, car-clogged, senile-retiree highway to hell that is the 111.

So long, it's been good to know ya

Wehrlissimo had reserved a spot for us at a froo-froo wine bar, and we rolled up to sandwiches, water, chips, and lots of wine. As each group of finishers passed us by, from our perch on the sidewalk we shouted "You're weak!" to the broken, salt-encrusted, beaten down cyclotourists.

Suddenly one of the freddies commanded, "Everyone! Stick your finger in your left ear!" Too drunk, frightened, tired, or confused to object, we all did as we were told.

"Remove fingers!"

We did.

"Inspect fingers!"

We looked at our fingertips, which were coated with an eighth of an inch layer of sand and grit stuck together with earwax. This, then, was our souvenir from Palm Springs, finer than any blue and yellow jersey designed by a middle schooler who "wanted to be an artist and was getting pretty good at Photoshop."

We said our goodbyes and Captain Doolittle proved again that he was the real man among men, and we lycra-clad fakers were precisely that. He'd not only flown the plane and ridden a hundred hard miles, but he'd abstained from so much as a sip of alcohol and looked like he'd hardly exerted himself. Oh, and he got us there and back alive.

Back on the tarmac in L.A., we deplaned and said our goodbyes. I thanked Wehrlissimo for his incredible generosity and offered him fifteen dollars to help pay for gas. "Thanks," he said, refusing my offer.

"So how much does a tank of airplane fuel cost for one of these trips, anyway?" I asked.

"About seven hundred dollars."

"Oh," I said, digging for an extra fiver.

He laughed. "All this stuff," he said, waving at the airplane and hangar, "isn't worth anything if you can't share it with your friends."

THE BABY DOLPHIN SLAUGHTER

Wankmeister got a text message from New Girl, who had just checked in with Fussy, Sparkles, Pilot, Canyon Bob, and Junkyard at Fess Parker's Doubletree Resort in Santa Barbara. "We're so excited about the Solvang Century tomorrow!" she texted. "Where are you staying?"

"Fess Parker's was booked by the time I called," Wanky replied. "That's the place named after the movie star who played Davy Crockett and Daniel Boone, right?"

"Right!"

"It's swankville, right?"

"Yep!"

"Well , the only place I could get was at Fess Haggen's."

"Fess Haggen's? Never heard of it."

"It's a smallish place named after Festus Haggen, the illiterate, dirty, alcoholic deadbeat who played Matt Dillon's deputy in Gunsmoke. They offered me their last room, out behind the dumpsters. I had to pass. So I'm flying in tomorrow with Wehrlissimo & Co."

"The same guys you did Palm Springs with?"

"Same bunch of wankers."

Culture and fitness, all rolled into one

Solvang, California is the picturesque Danish town made famous by Lance Armtwister and the U.S. Pestal Team when they won twelve consecutive Tours without ever doping. Remember when 190-lb. "Twiggy" Hincappy beat 115-lb. "Tubs" Pereiro on the 15th stage of the Tour in 2005, climbing 15,000 vertical feet over twelve major Alpine passes? That was thanks to the hard efforts the team spent in their Solvang winter training camp, and neither he nor Armtwister ever tested positive, despite being the most-tested athletes in the history of athletedom.

Like any other ethnic "town" (think "Chinatown" in San Francisco, or "Little Tokyo" in L.A., or Houston's "Cheap Hookers and Meth Village") Solvang introduces people to Danish culture without the inconvenience and expense of having to actually learn Danish and go to the Faroe Islands to watch a baby dolphin slaughter.

"What's this?" you say. "Danish people don't slaughter baby dolphins! That's Canadians. And they only slaughter baby seals. Danish people bake yummy butter cookies and have that precious statue of the Little Mermaid!"

Solvang does in fact promote enticing aspects of Danish cuisine, and numerous places in town exist where you can enjoy a yummy *frokost* of pickled herring, smoked eel, fried onions, smoked herring with raw egg yolk and saltmeat. For *middag* you can look forward to more salted fish, boiled potatoes, cabbage, rødgrød, and an appetizer of hot porridge. Yet, despite the great food, the high point of the town's celebration of Danish culture remains the annual baby dolphin hunt, carried out in the guise of a century ride.

The baby dolphin round-up

As with the Faroese dolphin hunt, Solvang first attracts the baby dolphins with offers of great weather, beautiful scenery, a memorial patch, and lots of overpriced five-dollar beer with outrageously overpriced twenty-dollar barbecue in the sunshine. When Wankmeister's crew of leathery whalers stepped off Wehrlissimo's turboprop, "The Dolphin Slaughter Express," and pedaled into Solvang from the Santa Ynez airpark, it was evident that the round-up had been a huge success.

Thousands of baby dolphins milled around the sign-in area, greedily looking through their goodie bags, happily taping their numbers to their handlebars, and proudly admiring the new "Solvang 2012" patch that they would never arrive home with to sew onto their jerseys. Some happily munched on the free nutty Clif bar included "free" with the sixty dollar entry fee, while others adjusted their tummies to rest comfortably on their top tubes. None was aware of the predators in their midst or the mayhem that would shortly ensue.

As the cold-eyed hunters from the South Bay hungrily gazed out at the roiling ocean of clueless cetaceans, some took the opportunity to sharpen their *sóknarønguls*, checking to make sure that the steel point of the gaff would sink quickly through the blubbery skin and into the brain of their prey. Given that the baby dolphins' brains were tiny indeed, the hunters' aim would have to be true. DJ, the Chief Hunter & Drunk, looked grimly at what would soon be a mass of lifeless corpses.

King Harald Bluetooth, slightly more humane, had opted to bring his *blásturongul* instead, preferring the blunt-edged gaff as an easier way to hook the unsuspecting baby dolphins by their blowholes, drag them to shore, beach them, cut their dorsal fins, and slice their spinal cords with an heirloom *grindaknívur*, handed down from father to son to bond the generations with the joyous, bloody murder of squeaking baby dolphins.

As the harpooners donned their own rider ID numbers, the better to blend with their victims, they noticed out in the parking lot a particularly plump batch of chubby little dolphin pups. Clad in Long Beach Mercury Poisoning outfits, they huddled together, comparing swag sack goodies and admiring each others' night-before boastful emails.

"Heh, heh," squeaked one baby dolphin. "I told the South Bay fakers about my one-hour massage and carbo loading! Katy bar the door!"

"Ho, ho," squeaked another, who had called

in from Long Beach on his iPhone because he was too weak to make the swim. "I'll post a funny blog afterwards when someone tells me about the ride I was too weak and craven to join!"

"Har, har," squeaked the last, "they're about to find out how the Long Beach baby dolphins roll!"

How the Long Beach baby dolphins roll

Under the command of their Chief Hunter & Drunk, the South Bay whalers left the safety of Solvang Bay and headed out to open sea with the group of tubby Long Beach dolphins in tow. The hunters of steely mien included King Harald Bluetooth, Wehrlissimo "Gorm the Old," Major Bob "Sweyn Forkbeard," Li'l Douggie "Sigrid the Haughty," Triple "Olaf Hunger," Polly "Cnut the Great," and ProBoy Alex "Sigrid the Dainty."

By mile four the rotating paceline of South Bay whalers had already hooked, beached, and severed the spinal cords of several thousand baby dolphins, most of whom were wobbling along in ill-defined schools led by someone wearing a jersey that said, "Winner — California Triple Crown of Cycling," whatever that was.

By mile five the Long Beach cetaceans had already begun to swim in panic mode, with Dr. Dave wildly squeaking out "Flat! Wheel change! Mechanical!" The largest of the blubbery mammals, a juvenile female pilot whale named Martijn the Feeble, called the school to a halt while everyone gathered around the quivering Dr. Dave. No one was able to find a flat or any problem whatsoever, but he insisted. "The wheel was wobbling! I swear!"

Harald Bluetooth looked scornfully and said, "The wheel was wobbling because your arms were shaking, dude. Okay, let's go."

The cold bite of the lance

At mile thirty-seven one of the fattest baby dolphins, after taking numerous pulls, swung over to the side, his flippers quaking from the effort. "Thar she blows!" roared Gorm the Old as he took out his long harpoon and sent the steely blade of death piercing directly to the heart of the hapless mammal. Gore coursed from his mouth, then from his eyes and nose as the helpless creature rolled over, white belly to the sun, jaws agape in the final shudder of death. No more to enjoy the depths of the ocean blue! No more to swim among the chubby schools of baby dolphins, spouting boastful emails! No more to carbo-load the night before being driven onto the beach to be slain by the pitiless iron tip of the harpooner's lance!

By mile forty practically the entire pod of Long Beach baby dolphins had had the sharp end of the gaff driven through their blowholes, with the exception of Martijn the Feeble, Ross the Tenacious, and Craig the Dubious, the latter two of whom were more swimming reptiles than fish. The entirety of the South Bay whaling contingent remained. At one point in the hunt King Harald Bluetooth dropped back to assist Gorm the Old, whose boat sprang a leak and needed a tow back up to the main fleet. Tube Top, one of the smaller hermaphroditic baby dolphins whose penis was not large or well formed enough to differentiate his genitalia from that of the females, made the fatal mistake of holding onto King Harald's tow line even after Sigrid the Haughty had driven the tip of the harpoon deep into Tube Top's innards, penetrating his uterus and coming out through his left flipper. As he sank beneath the foamy brine he was heard to cry, "Why am I so weak?"

Though the Long Beach dolphins had for the most part been easily dispatched owing to the high concentrations of mercury in their livers, a vile and thoroughly inedible group of Simple Green invertebrate suckerfish, along with a trio of Canyon Verde gasbag puffer minnows had latched onto the fast-traveling whaling vessel.

Although Martijn the Feeble tried to dislodge them with shouts of "Pull through, you pussies!" it became clear that you cannot appeal to the pride of parasitic life forms who have none. At this very moment a stiff sea breeze sprang up in the form of a howling crosswind, driving the frenzied fish into the troughs of the waves where they could easily be isolated and where the bloody point of death could easily be driven through their miniature brains. They were not seen again.

The hunters stopped at the halfway mark in

Santa Maria to re-sharpen their gaffs, and a small contingent of mortally wounded baby Long Beach dolphins floundered in, trailing blood and entrails. They would expire shortly after the hunting resumed.

As the sailors left the harbor, it became apparent that many of the sturdy South Bay harpooners, tired after such a bloody and successful harvest, were less than eager to begin rowing again in earnest. Worse, the skulking and resilient female pilot whale, Martijn the Feeble, despite her sagging tummy and poorly attached feminine hygiene pads, was proving difficult to kill.

Wankmeister saw an opportunity and easily rowed away, confident that Martijn the Feeble would never close the gap, especially since the remaining heroes were almost exclusively from the South Bay. For thirty miles he toiled, now alone, now rowing with other castaways, now joining a soon-to-be-wrecked armada of riders from Orange County.

Unfortunately, the unthinkable had occurred. The Chief Hunter & Drunk had made a pact with the Feeble One of the Sagging Paunch and Ross the Reptile, while the remaining whalers joined forces to row down their valiant and heroic companion. As with most perfidious plans, this one caused terrible destruction within the South Bay contingent, as the catch came just before the Straits of Foxen.

Calamity in the deep

Although the baby dolphins had long ago

been harpooned, skinned, doused with spit and piss, and consigned to ignominy, catastrophe now overtook the hunters, as one by one they dashed in their hulls and floundered in the pounding surf. Wankmeister rowed valiantly but to no avail as the Paunchy One, the Chief Drunk & Traitor, and ProBoy Backstabber made their escape.

Once through the straits, however, and despite the fatigue of his godlike thirty-mile escape, Wankmeister overtook ProBoy and, rejoined by Harald Bluetooth, began a furious chase. But who of this world can run down the Chief Hunter & Drunk when he rows in anger knowing that beer is near at hand, even when he is dragging the useless and snot-encrusted baggage of Martijn the Feeble?

Just as Wankmeister contemplated the futility of the chase, they hit the Foxen Shoals, a devastatingly rocky passage just beyond the straits. ProBoy leaped ahead followed by Harald, as Wankmeister was humiliatingly passed by a chubby husband and wife who had set out the night before and were wearing matching Google bicycling outfits.

Stung by the triple mortification of losing to the Feeble One, being dropped by ProBoy, and facing death at the hands of two baby Googlefish, WM nutted up, rejoined Bluetooth after a powerful chase, then caught and shelled ProBoy, who as punishment had to go race the Tour of India and the Criterium Nationale de Burundi.

King Harald Bluetooth and Wankmeister

poured on the coal, coming to within two hundred yards of the Chief Traitor and the She-whale, who were easily tracked by the trail of snot that the She-whale had left upon the billows. The chasers' efforts came to naught. Once through the last reef, the Chief Traitor opened up a gap so huge and in the middle of such a vicious crosswind that the chasers simply gave up, beaten in spirit, exhausted of body, and wholly incapable of reeling in the dastardly duo.

When Wankmeister and Harald came in some two minutes adrift with broken oars and tattered sails, the Traitor and the She-whale laughed in contempt. "You," crowed the whale, "are weak!"

Truer words, on this day at least, were never spoken...at least by her.

P[u]CK[e]RR

The phone rang. It was Fukdude. "You wanna do the 35+ race on Saturday? Eighty-seven miles. Five thousand feet of climbing."

"Where is it?"

"Santa Barbara. It's an easy race, but it'll be a beatdown for you. You probably won't finish. Four hours in the saddle. Davy Dawg's going."

"What about Fireman?"

"Nah. He got dropped on the first climb last year. It's not even a climb."

"Santa Barbara? That's all day. Plus gas money, food, entry fee, coffee, more food, Advil. Almost a hundred bucks to go get my head staved in?"

"Fuck yeah, dude. You in?"

"Sure."

Fukdude only speaks the truth

I showed up at his place at 7:15. He ushered me in, poured me a cup of coffee and seated me at the breakfast table. Chloe jumped up, landed on my nuts and shed four coats of fur in my lap. "Get down Chloe, fucking dog. Hey dude, something unfucking believably good is going to happen to you today."

I perked up. I'd been training hard and my

legs were starting to come around. "Yeah?" I tried not to look too eager.

"Fuck yeah, dude. Homemade baked chocolate donuts. The fucking bomb." He pulled a fresh donut out of the oven and slathered it with a two-inch layer of chocolate frosting. "Fucking eat that, dude. Best thing that's going to happen to you today, unless you have a second one. It's all fucking downhill from there."

I ate the donut. Then another. We polished off an even dozen and emptied the can of frosting by taking turns running our fingers inside the can. "Fucking rad shit, huh?" he said with enthusiasm. "Okay dude, let's go fucking race."

Race with your legs, win with your head

"This race is a fucking joke," Fukdude said after we'd picked up his dad, who was going to recover from last week's major surgery by standing in the ninety-degree heat for four hours to hand us water bottles. "The break goes in the first five miles. Then the pack just stands on its dick at thirteen mph the rest of the day. Same thing every fucking year."

Dawg nodded. "It's pretty easy. The lane is super narrow and the centerline rule is enforced, so after the break goes, the lane clogs and you can't advance. It's a clusterfuck. Super lame layout. Last year it finished in a huge downhill that guaranteed mass crashes. What do you expect from something designed by college kids?"

"I don't know. Beer stops along the way?"

"I wish," said Dawg.

"So here's the fucking plan, dude. There's only three of us so we're like total non-factors. The break will go quick. One of us will cover the first break, and when it comes back another one of us goes with the counterattack. If the counter gets pulled back, the last one of us goes with the next counter. Just don't tard out and miss the fucking break. Stage up front and stay up front. Ride aggressive and hammer but don't be a dork and pull the whole field up with you. It's like this every year, dude."

"Wasn't it shorter last year?" I asked.

"Yeah, it was only fifty-eight miles last year. And this year THOG, the Unmeek, Glasship, a couple of other national champions and ex-pros will be racing it. So it could be a beatdown for you. Probably will be, I mean."

Timing is everything

"How much farther?" asked Dawg after we'd been in the car for a very long time.

"Forty miles it looks like."

"But our race starts in an hour and we're only going fifty."

"Fuck dude, I've never missed a race start in twenty years. Came close, though. Me and Vince and Fireman and some other dude wound up at the wrong place one time, twenty miles away and we all had to piss like crazy but we didn't have time so we just passed around an empty plastic jug and Vince was the last pisser, fucking jug was sloshing with a half gallon of warm piss and this old guy steps off the curb in front of the van just when Vince is in full dam release mode and I hit the fucking brakes and he drops the jug and the fucking van is bam! Filled with piss and it was just fucking nasty. I had to pull over I was laughing so fucking hard. Plus our kits and shoes and helmets all got soaked. But we made the fucking start."

We got there, signed in, got our numbers, and lined up with ten minutes to spare with no piss on us anywhere.

I looked at the starters and realized that of the ones I recognized, they all had something in common: I'd never beaten any of them in a race or even on a training ride.

I also realized the difference between a road race and a crit. In a crit you have the illusion that you have a chance of winning. Everyone finishes together and you can't get dropped unless you completely give up. Even Clotts could finish a crit when he was almost three hundred pounds, and once he finally slimmed down to two-fifty he was winning.

At a long, hot road race with hills there is no illusion of success. If you are a fat sprinter you will get dropped. Once you get dropped you will flail by yourself until you quit or you experience systemic organ failure. Your chance of winning is zero. That's zero with a zero in front and behind. This is the reason that lots of hacker road racers do crits, sucked in by the false illusion that they might somehow win, but no self-respecting crit racer ever pins on a number at a hard, hilly road race. There is no chance of winning, and worse, not even the illusion that it's possible. And worse, they tack on DNF next to your name after you quit so when everyone checks the results online the next day they all say "Tsk-tsk, that dork's a crit racer. No way he was gonna finish that race. What was he thinking?" The thought that you could have spent your $45 entry fee and $59 in gas money on beer while watching cycling videos at home is the arsenic icing on a shit cake.

Blessed as I was with an overly active fantasy life, I could imagine victory in even the most completely hopeless situations, which this would quickly turn out to be. Moreover, I didn't have to come home and explain defeat to my wife and kids, because it always went like this.

"Hi, honey, I'm home."

"You lookin' onna awful. Getting' beaten again and givin' it up?"

"Yep."

"You not onna learn. Take a shower you smellin' bad an you make onna your own peanuts butter sandwich."

Executing the strategy

Three minutes into the eighty-seven mile deathfest a LaGrange wanker attacked. Fukdude went

with him. I was in the front row while the field led a
steady tempo chase. As we crested the first "non-hill"
that had shredded Fireman and Vince the year before,
I was at six hundred watts and seeing triple. "This is
the easy part?" I thought.

We bombed the descent and the peloton
reeled in the break. A couple of counterattacks
followed. I went with each one and tasted the howling
headwind and stabbing leg pains for the handful of
seconds we were free. My legs felt great but this didn't
really seem like the race Fukdude had described. I'd
already hit 1041 watts following one counterattack.
No break had stuck for more than a few minutes and
we were fifteen miles into the race.

Since the race was out and back on Foxen
Canyon Road, every couple of minutes we were
buffeted by a huge clump of racers from races that
had started before ours going the opposite direction,
many of whom were over the centerline with their
heads down, which created lots of excitement with
guys in our peloton who were also over the centerline
with their heads down.

In addition, the road was packed with regular
car traffic going to and from the various wineries in
the area, so all the motorists were drunk and the
remaining vehicles were farm trucks or duallies
hauling extra wide trailers filled with pipes that
projected over the sides. The turnaround was a super
tight U-turn in the already narrow road that funneled
eighty flailing racers into a tiny chute, so unless you

were in the top five you had to unclip or risk tipping over or whacking into the bike in front of you.

After the U-turn there came a mad acceleration and a furious flurry of attacks that launched the winning break. With the jumps and the wind and the fighting for position, by the time we hit the only Fukdude Certified "real climb," which was the backside of Foxen Canyon that we'd descended on the way out, my legs were shot.

Time for Plan B, as in "Beatdown"

As the real racers stretched their legs on the short but steep climb, the detritus in the rear looked like it was being mowed down by a perfectly positioned marksman with a machine gun. Riders flailed off to the edge of the road. Shoulders heaved. Heads slumped. Strange body positions erupted as wankers with redlined heart rates found new contorted ways to thrash and beat and flog the pedals.

I got shelled and watched my wattage drop back down to 320, a number I don't even see doing intervals. I crested the top and then chased like a madman. A huge group of Harleys had come up from the rear along with several farm trucks, and I flew along at forty-five mph, weaving and dodging and drafting my way back up to the lead group, choking on diesel and gasoline exhaust as my bike skittered on the loose gravel and my body shook from the jarring hits on the potholes and cracked pavement. I thanked Dog that this was an easy race. I wondered, but only briefly, why I'd just risked my life in order to catch back up to a race I had no chance of winning and little chance of even finishing. What about my children? What about my wife? What about my responsibilities?

The answer of course was "That's why you have two mil in accidental death."

At the feed zone, which the dumb college kids had put right at the new uphill finish, I slowed to get water and as a result got dropped by the accelerating pack. I chased on just in time to go up the Fukdude Certified Nonhill, barely making it over with the pack. Having recalibrated my goal to "just finish," I slid to the back and tried to sit in.

Until that point I'd been fighting to hold position or fighting to advance through the bar-to-bar knot of riders, and in addition to being stuck on the edge of the group I was always catching wind, my hands aching from the constant braking, and I was at wit's end from the exhaustion of trying to advance.

Once I gave up and surrendered myself to the languor of hopelessness and defeat by sliding to the rear, it was peaceful. The pace had dropped considerably ever since the breakaway had sailed, and we now rode at a leisurely crawl except for one horrific moment when we overtook the entire 45+ field. Imagine two beginner marching bands, one composed of nothing but tubas and the other composed of extension ladders and grappling hooks, overtaking each other at full tilt on a narrow strip of land, either side of which dropped into a moat filled with crocodiles.

I thought of Fukdude's contempt for this lame pace and could only disagree with him. This slowness was awesome. Unfortunately, as we slowed down, the overtaken 45+ field ramped it up, and the tuba-ladder band thing happened again, with a couple of our tubas mixing with their ladders and splattering riders all over the pavement. As I cowered and refused to take risks I reminded myself how slowly bones heal, how long skin grafts take, and how painful neck fractures are once you're over forty-five.

Different strokes for different folks

Just before the turnaround on the second lap, Glass Hip floated to the back. "Hey, Wankmeister," he said with a grin. "How's it going?" Before I could answer, he said, "Is this a lame race or what? If it were any easier I'd have brought my grandmother along, and she's been dead for ten years."

At that exact moment I felt like I was at the bottom of the Marianas Trench with ten thousand tons of deep-sea manganese nodules pressing down on my balls. "Uh, I'm wrecked, dude. I don't know if I'm going to finish."

"Ever the comedian!" he laughed, and easily pedaled back up to the front.

On the second time up the steep hill the machine gunner had been replaced by men with large clubs. Every few riders they would select a victim, bash in his head and leave him where he fell without even the courtesy of a common grave and a sack of quicklime. The carnage was unbelievable.

Team Carmen's, which had shown up in full force with their A Team, all of whom were fully equipped with new rigs and Di2 transmissions, lost riders left and right. As I came unhitched again I dropped into the 320-watt range and passed Elbows. I had never passed Elbows anywhere. He looked like he'd just finished a bad Scientology session with Tom Cruise. He wasn't on my team but he was a great guy, and I'd never forget the time we broke away at Lunada Bay on the Donut Ride and he towed me to the college, waving me ahead in the last few meters for the win.

"Get on my wheel, buddy," I urged.

He gurgled something, latched on, and I dragged him over the top. Then it was a repeat of lap one: Full-on chase in the hope we could latch back onto the main pack. This time we overtook Davy Dawg, who was flailing like a lost puppy. He hopped on, took a deep breath, and singlehandedly dragged us the remaining three miles up to the main group.

When we hit the feed zone Elbows crumbled like a cookie baked with too much flour and not enough milk, wobbled off the course and out of the race. It looked like a perfect move, and since the group had dropped me again in the feed zone I too made a beeline for the Give Up and Shamelessly Quit Zone.

Just as I tried to exit, Walshy, who was sitting on the side of the road, yelled at me. "C'mon, Wanky! You can catch them!"

Too embarrassed to quit and too frightened to say "No, I can't," I made the U-turn and chased. And chased. And chased.

The chase of the wank brigade

After a long time that seemed even longer, in that special here-I-am-endlessly-in-hell time warp that you fall into when hopelessly off the back of a long road race, I overhauled Davy Dawg, who had gotten shelled again, and we picked up the stragglers, the wounded, the beaten, the dropped, the Left Behinds, and formed a rag-tag wank brigade. Two miles up the road was the lead group of perhaps thirty riders, followed by six of us and one droppee from the 45+ Elderly Gentlemen's race.

When we hit the bottom of the hill for the last time everyone was fried. Granted, we were the wank brigade. Granted, we were now fighting for the best placing of the final six, which is to say the worst of everyone else. Granted, no one cared. Granted, the only thing anyone wanted was to finish.

When you're an aged flailing bicycle racer, though, and you've paid a bunch of money (more than fifteen bucks), and you've traveled all day, and you're dehydrated, and you have a pounding headache, and you're fifteen years older than the next youngest guy, and you're used to getting dropped and riding by yourself, and you're in the incredible position of actually, possibly finishing a 35+ leg-breaking road race...it matters. So I attacked at the bottom of the hill and gloriously soloed in for my close-to-bottom-of-the-barrel-placing. It was the hardest race I could remember having finished and the best placing I could reasonably expect for what remains in this lifetime.

For every action there is an equal and opposite reaction

The kidneys serve essential regulatory roles in the urinary system and also serve homeostatic functions such as the regulation of electrolytes, regulation of blood pressure, filtration of the blood, removal of wastes, and the reabsorption of water, glucose, and amino acids.

Symptoms of renal failure — which results in death — include vomiting, diarrhea, nausea, weight loss, dark colored urine, blood in the urine, difficulty urinating, itching, bone damage, muscle cramps, hypocalcaemia, abnormal heart rhythms, muscle paralysis, swelling of the extremities, shortness of breath, as well as pain in the back and sides. When I got off my bike I experienced all of these symptoms at once, plus a grinding headache so intense that I would have done anything to make it go away, including another lap around the course.

Fukdude and Davy Dawg, although tired, were jocular. "You're looking kind of pale, Wanky. Let's get you a cheeseburger and some beer."

Fukdude knew that any race day beginning with chocolate donuts was required to end with cheeseburgers and beer.

Soon enough we were at the Firestone Brewery, seated with G$ who had also done the race, and his lovely parents from North Carolina. I introduced myself with a brief story about my great-great grandfather John Turner from Wilmington and the mule he was given by Robert E. Lee at Appomattox, and then I collapsed with my face in the patty melt.

Mrs. G$ looked at her son. "Does he do this often?"

"Talk about his great-grandfather? Nope, that's the first time I've heard that story. But he does look like this after most bike races."

Dawg chimed in. "This is actually perky for him." He snapped a photo and posted it on Facebook. "He usually collapses before we get to the restaurant."

Back in the van I napped for a couple of hours and nursed a couple of gels given to me by Fukdude. In time, I rallied.

"Dude, that was a fucking hard race," said Fukdude.

"Yeah, that was a beatdown," added Dawg.

I thought about the morning's baked donuts. "You were right, Kev."

"About what?"

"About the best part of the day."

"Donuts were fucking rad, eh? First race is always a fucking beatdown. Boulevard road race is next weekend. You in, bro?"

I paused to dry heave into a plastic bag. "Fuck, yeah."

WELCOME TO HELL

Everything was going fine. There we were, whizzing along at forty-six mph in a tightly grouped bunch of grizzled codgers, when we rounded a modestly tight bend. Zing! Perky floated across the center line (bad), locked up the brakes (worse), and went flying headfirst into a tree (worst).

A collective "Thank Dog it's not me" shuddered through the peloton as some of Perky's Big Orange teammates looked with concern, briefly, in the direction of his crumpled body. Suddenly, things no longer seemed fine and a concatenation of worries flashed across my mind.

"What am I doing here? Why are elderly men with prostate issues crashing their bikes into trees at fifty miles per hour? How am I going to get this embrocation off my balls?"

Then I realized it. Weird shit always happens at the Boulevard Road Race and Social Hour.

The race stages a mile or so down the hill from the Golden Acorn Casino, which is a good name for the opportunities that await at the road race. The acorn is a tiny little booger, and even if it were solid gold, it would barely be worth a couple hundred bucks — about the prize money you could expect to win for one of the road race events if you took all top ten placings. And of course for most of the seventy some-odd idiots who signed up for the 45+ race, the chance of winning was slimmer than getting a twenty-five dollar payout at the Golden Acorn.

Unlike the previous year, when I planned a convincing win but instead got dropped halfway up the four-mile climb on the first lap, my goals this year were more modest. I would be happy to finish the first lap with the leaders. Everything else would be gravy. And after watching Perky climb that tree on his bike, I added "finish without hitting a tree" to the list.

In the staging area, wedged between the double-wides and the single toilet provided for the quaking bowels of all three hundred racers, I took stock of the competition. There was the short fat guy in the painted-on skinsuit. "What is that wanker doing here? Didn't he get the memo about the six-mile climb followed by the four-mile climb followed by the paramedic tent? Idiot."

There was the big, tall, fat guy lathered in tattoos and wearing a half-polka dotted maroon kit from Team Dude Chick. "Did he take a wrong turn looking for the transvestite bar? This is a road race, a hard one for hard men you dreamer. Go home now and save the entry fee, for Dog's sake!"

Over there was a gnome with crooked legs and triple-bent spine. "The nursing home is back in El Cajon. Maybe they let him out of the Alzheimer's ward for the day to play the slots and he wandered down here by mistake?"

These few minutes of rolling around in the bright sunshine reminded me that, sunshine or not, we were still at four thousand feet and it wouldn't take much for the sixty-degree weather to plummet the moment we left the protection of the valley. Something like, say, a howling wind, which there appeared to be, judging from the wildly spinning wind turbines up on the hill.

Moments before the gun sounded, a Breakaway from Cancer rider shouted out, "Hey! Listen up! Today is Glass Hip's birthday! Let's sing him a chorus of 'Happy Birthday!'" At first everyone thought it was a joke, and then the wisecracks started. "What about a chorus of 'You're So Vain?'"

After the jeers subsided, seventy raspy voices broke into a half-hearted rendition of the birthday classic. Glass Hip, touched all the way down to his artificial joint, allowed as how he'd "Never been more prettily serenaded by an uglier group of post-menopausal guys." And off we went, thirty of us to a bike race, another thirty-nine of us to a one-or-two lap beatdown followed by an early withdrawal, and me to my doom.

When we hit the bottom of the long climb on the first lap my legs felt great. A nasty acceleration at the front strung us out and summarily dropped everyone who hadn't already quit or run into a tree. I smiled to myself. "Is this the best these alleged national and former world champions have? Puh-leeze."

Halfway up the climb, almost exactly where I'd come off the year before, a rather unpleasant sensation began building up in my legs. In seconds it had spread to my lungs, throat, head, and finally my eyes. In a few more seconds I watched the lead group ride away.

Without the shelter of the group there was a vicious, horribly cold headwind. I crumpled as the long line of shellees pushed on by. After the world's longest mile we reattached to the lead, and I remembered that part of my pre-game nutrition plan had been to eat one peanut butter-flavored mouthful of Barbie food per lap.

The pace had slowed and I reached into my jersey and fished out a BonkBreaker. I'm not sure why, but they are housed in wrapping that is easy to open with a blowtorch, but impossible to tear into with your teeth.

Starving, terrified that a bonk was near, and too tightly wedged into the pack to take both hands off the bars (I could see the headline now: Cat 3 Wanker Loses Control of Bike Trying to Open Candy Wrapper, Kills Great American Cycling Dog Thurlow Rogers), I wrestled one-handed with the packaging.

The harder I bit and pulled, the more it didn't open, until in desperation I was jerking so hard that I could feel my back molars start to wiggle in their sockets. This headline wasn't much better: 45+ Wanker Pulls All Rear Teeth out of Gums in Epic Battle for Lump of Peanut Butter.

All this pulling through clenched teeth meant that no air had been getting to my lungs. Now it was either open the package or pass out. The wrapper finally tore and in a flash I had half the thick, dry, lumpy treat in my mouth. A simultaneous, massive inhalation almost rammed the food down my windpipe, but at the last second I wrestled it over to the side of my mouth with my tongue.

The oxygen debt created by the wrapper battle was huge, and I gasped as I tried to gulp down enough air without choking on the treat. Unable to chew, my spit soaked the brown peanut butter candy lump and dissolved part of it. Before I could swallow the liquefied part of the goop we hit the sharp climb through the aptly named "feed zone." Now on the tail of the lead group and coming unhitched, it was impossible to do anything but suck desperately for air. Having gone to this much effort to get the Barbie food into my mouth, I wasn't about to spit it out. Instead, the violent exhalations forced the dark brown spitgoop out of the corners of my mouth, along my cheeks and down my chin.

Thrust up against the line of shouting spectators, each person saw me from mere inches away as I labored by. "Oh my God," I heard one horrified woman say. "He's vomiting up his own shit!"

The people in front of her looked as I came by, my face contorted in pain. A little boy stared, fascinated and happy, as the brown chunks began to spill out.

"And he's trying to swallow it back down, too!" This was perhaps the grimmest headline of all: "45+ Wanker Pukes up Own Feces, Re-Eats It to Survive Mindlessly Hard Road Race."

At the top of the feed zone the pack had left me again. And unlike last year when I'd had a few dropaway companions to slog along with, this time I was alone with forty-two miles to go and a freezing headwind to contend with. Suddenly, who should whiz by but the wizened gnome from the staging area. Mr. Gnomes was on a mission, and unbeknownst to him, part of his mission was about to include me.

I hopped onto Gnomes's wheel and he lit into the downhill. The leaders were in sight and he was determined to catch. We raced into the stretch where the road began to rise again and there, on the side of the road, was No Quarter Flagg from Big Orange, changing a rear wheel. "Poor bastard," I thought. "He's gonna be flailing by himself out here on the course for the rest of the race. He'll never catch us."

Mr. Gnomes railed us to within two hundred yards of the pack and then swung over for me to close the last bit of pavement. I pulled heroically for a few seconds before my legs returned to their rubbery state. Gnomes came through and charged as hard as he could, then popped, and the leaders vanished around the bend.

It was going to be a very long day, and I started thinking about starting up a conversation with

Mr. Gnomes. Just as I'd hit upon an icebreaker, I heard the sound of whizzing carbon rims. In a flash we were passed by Flagg. I leaped for his wheel, realizing that he, too, was on a mission, and that his mission, if properly utilized, could include me. Mr. Gnomes, after nobly helping me this far and sacrificing himself for a complete stranger, was left pitilessly behind. I came close to feeling sorry for him, a little.

Flagg was going unbearably fast when he came by, but upon hitting the downhill he really opened up the jets. Occasionally looking back to see if I would help with the effort, he soon realized that he was dragging the deadest of deadwood. Somehow Mr. Gnomes time trailed back on, and the two of them smashed and bashed and beat the pedals to a fare-thee-well while I thanked them from the bottom of my heart.

After a couple of miles we started seeing the taillights from the lead motorcycle just around the next curve, and another mile later the entire 45+ field was right there. A more beautiful sight I have never seen, naked beautiful women included, and to make matters sweeter I had been dragged back up to the main field without having to do a lick of work. Mr. Gnomes was starting to pedal squares but I figured I'd wait until they were proper triangles before relieving him with a pull.

We caught the pack at the railroad tracks and the final effort up that sharp bump was too much for

Gnomes, who shattered and fell back, never to see the leaders again. I felt profound sorrow for him as I straggled onto the rear. Poor Mr. Gnomes. He was such a good fellow and such a hard worker, and he had done so much to resuscitate my race. To be dumped mercilessly by a freeloading wheelsuck like me just at the moment of success, it was almost too much for me to think about, so I didn't.

A few seconds passed and the road began to rise. The Tragedy of Gnomes evaporated from my mind and the Execution of Wanky, Act II, came to the fore. Flagg had caught his breath and shot to the front. "That," I said, "is exactly what I must do. Shoot to the front. Because it's dangerous here in the back, where the slightest acceleration will cause me to get immediately shelled."

I shot to the front and relaxed in safety amongst the rainbow and red-white-blue collars and sleeves. The road rose again. With a power and speed that amazed even me, I shot backwards as the inevitable acceleration came. And I kept shooting, all the way out the back, for good. The pack rolled away.

In the next few miles I became acquainted with a kindly gentleman who by day was a sociologist and statistician. We exchanged pleasantries before he most unpleasantly dropped me and rode away. Two other riders came by. I tried to engage them in conversation but they had better places to be than a windswept, barren desert climb a few miles from the Mexican border that hid armed drug smugglers, with the sun quickly going down and a whiff of hypothermia in the air.

On the long climb I was even passed by Ol' Grizzles, the aged, mustachioed chap with dense, furry legs. He encouraged me with a "Come on, buddy!" but he would have gotten a better reaction from one of the large boulders on the side of the road.

Back in the feed zone people eyed me strangely. I crested the hill and Mr. Gnomes came by. "Fuck this shit," he said. "I'm done."

With an entire lap remaining I was about to be passed by the leaders in the Pro/1/2 field. Going up the next grade the referee slowed down his motor. "The Pro/1/2 field is coming."

"Am I the last 45+ racer?"

He raised his eyebrow at the self-description of "racer."

"What number series is your category? 500's? Nah, you're not last. There are still quite a few spread out over the course behind you."

This was the shot in the arm that would get me around the course. With a hard enough effort I might finish 26th, improving an entire placing over the previous year! It sure made the thousands of dollars in equipment upgrades, the countless hours in the morning at 5:00 AM doing intervals before work, and the $700 monthly coaching fee seem worth it.

I sprunted up the climb and dropped into the long downhill. Along came the Pro/1/2 field and the follow motor. Behind the motorcycle was the short fat guy with the painted on skinsuit who I'd secretly laughed at in the staging area. I hopped on his wheel, not laughing so much anymore. We drafted the motor as long as we could, which wasn't nearly long enough.

We crossed the railroad tracks and the fat guy dropped me. Next was the tattooed rider from Team Dude Chick. He was in dude mode. Although he looked too big to get up the grade without a helium balloon, he was amazingly fast, or I was amazingly slow, or both. He, too, left me before we could get a lively conversation going, which was quite unfriendly of him, it seemed.

Much, much later I finished. Incredibly, there were eight people slower and dumber than I. By now I was frozen to the bone, but not too frozen to stop and ask Glass Hip, who was changing a flat on his car, about the results of the race that I had been in but had not really been in.

THOG had won. G$ had gotten second. Glass Hip had destroyed the remnants of the field for third. Flagg got eighth. Glass Hip looked fresh and happy and relaxed, not like someone who'd just been to hell and decided to live there. "You okay, buddy? What's that brown stuff all over your face? You need a doctor?"

"I'll be fine. Thanks." The temperature had fallen into the thirties with the wind chill. It was almost dark. I stripped down in front of a double-wide then hopped into the car, cranking the heater full blast. I'd taken my two chances in the race, Mr. Slim and Mr. None, and wound up with the latter.

I took that as an omen and rolled on past the Golden Acorn casino, sorely tempted though I was to try my luck there. It was a long drive home.

UCLA ROAD RACE AND ASIAN LIBRARY RETREAT

The definition of insanity is doing the same thing over and over again but expecting a different result. The definition of bike racing is getting beaten down over and over again, and doing it over and over again.

The UCLA Road Race holds its annual festival of pedaling fun on the Devil's Punchbowl course, far from all those Asians in the library whose parents come and do their laundry. In fact, Punchbowl was recently rated the Least Asian-friendly Road Race Course in America, beating out Gruene, Texas, and Bakersfield, California, by a wide margin. You can listen to the UCLA Road Race Asian Theme Song on YouTube by searching for "Ching Chong Ling Long song."

This was my tenth attempt at a race held on the infamous Pukebowl course, a windblown, trash-strewn, barren wasteland of cactus, rusting trailer homes, sand, grit, meth incubators, and bad memories. I knew it was going to be bad this year, too, because it was always bad and because of the howling wind that picked up and blew away the sign-in tent. I also knew it was going to be bad because none of my teammates would ride to the race with me. Bike racers, in addition to their generally unscientific approach to racing ("I heard beta carotene will stop cramps,") are terribly superstitious. Once word gets out that you're a bad luck racer, even your teammates will stop offering you rides. In my case it had gotten so bad that the entire team refused to attend the race. "Dude, you're snakebit. The blogging is funny and all, but you're rat poison in the birthday cake. We're gonna ride the track and go drink some beers."

Tri-Dork to the rescue

Fortunately Tri-Dork knew nothing of this, and since, like most triathletes, he doesn't do great with long words and had therefore never read my blog, he agreed to give me a ride. It was his first road race and in exchange for taking me to the race I promised to give him free coaching advice on tactics.

As we got underway I began with Rule 1: Proper Pre-Race Nutrition. "You had lunch, dude?"

"Isn't it kind of early? It's only ten and we don't start until 1:30."

"Dude, it's probably too late. A triple cheeseburger and fries take almost four hours to properly digest."

He laughed nervously. "You're joking, right?"

"Yeah. Two hours is plenty."

"We never ate cheeseburgers before triathlons."

"And how many did you win?"

"Only a dozen or so, actually."

"QED. Hey, perfect timing. There's an In-N-Out!" He still hoped I might be joking. "Stop the car!" I ordered. Tri-Dork swung into the parking lot. Now he was scared.

Lunch of champions

As we sat down to our triple meat with sautéed onions, jalapeños, and large Coke, I explained. "Dude, you have zero chance in this race. You weigh a hundred and ninety pounds, not counting the five you're about to add. This race has six thousand feet of climbing over a fifty mile course and the next heaviest guy in the race is me at one sixty. Glass Hip is here; a buck fifty. G$ at one fifty-five. Baby 'DQ' Louie barely tips the scales at one thirty. You are going to get dropped immediately by the dwarves; you'll get shelled even faster than me. You're probably not going to finish once you're out there flogging by yourself up the face of a cliff in a howling sandstorm. So knowing that it's hopeless and that you suck, your only recourse is to drown your sorrow in greasy food. Chow down."

Rule 2: Proper pre-race psychology

As Tri-Dork guided the fully loaded Prius and the even more fully loaded us onto the highway, he asked me about race wheels. "These new Ksyriums are really light. I'm hoping they'll make a difference on the climb."

"Dude, that triple cheeseburger you just ate weighed more than your bike frame. If you want to do well in this race, which is impossible, you need to have the proper mental preparation."

Tri-Dork smiled. "I'm pretty good in that area. The year I got second at Kona I took an entire course on race psychology. The Ironman, after you have the fitness, is all in your head."

"Look, Kona is for pussies. It's a coffee blend, for Dog's sake. Triathlon has all the strategy of beating off: Start out easy, build up gradually, and make sure you save the final spurt for the end. Any fifteen year-old can figure that out. But you're bike racing now, Dorky. The mental aspect is completely different." I could tell the analogy had hit home because his confidence had cracked a tad and he looked worried.

"Okay. So what should I do?"

The bike-a-rama sutra

"If triathlon strategy is wanking, then bike racing strategy is sex. Which means a couple of things. First, you're number one; to hell with everyone else. Second, you gotta have the right equipment. Third, what you do depends on what the other person does. Fourth, you have options: Suck wheel, pound from the front, come from behind...it's complicated and takes practice. Sometimes you think you can shoot through the hole, but you have to pull back and go for a different opening.

"You also need to get in the right frame of mind by distrusting everyone in the race. Just like casual sex. Assume your partner has every disease in the book."

"Even my teammates?"

"Especially them. Just remember your only possible role on a team is to work for riders who are better than you. Which is all of them."

"Okay. So then what?"

"Once you recognize that the world is your enemy you must never take a pull. Ever. Sit on wheels. Hide from the front. Save everything for the two big moments of the race."

"What are those?"

"The first is when you get dropped. Save all your energy for making a lunge to close the gap."

"So I can get back on?"

"No. You'll never get back on. When they accelerate at the top of the climb, physics will overcome fantasy and you will become a giant millstone heaved off a tall cliff into a very deep lake."

"So why do I need to save my effort if I'm just going to get dropped?"

"So you can tell me after the race how close you were to hanging on. 'I was THIS close! Just a bike length!' By the way, 'just a bike length' when getting dropped on a climb is approximately equal to the distance that light travels in one year. Just so you know."

"This is complicated. What's the second big

moment?"

"The finish, where you put yourself through agonies unimaginable to the average forty-five year-old gentleman with prostate issues as you risk life, limb, and fifteen thousand dollars in race equipment to beat out some other wanker for 47th place."

Ol' Gizzards and comeback

We pawed the dirt at the starting line as I surveyed the competition. Glass Hip was looking relaxed, fit, and intimidating with his new death row crew-cut designed to minimize the fact that he was almost completely bald. The more he smiled and smalltalked with Baby 'DQ' Louie the more I realized how bitter this beatdown was going to be. G$ casually straddled his top tube, looking like a giant heart and lung with two long legs attached as an afterthought. Kalashnikov sat calmly, fresh blood from the roadkill he'd just eaten still dripping from his fangs. No Quarter Flagg, who at one-seventy was the true beast of the race, looked coolly at the race official.

Then I pinched myself. These guys weren't my competition. I'd never passed any of them at a stop light, much less in a race. My competition was Bumblebee, the newt in a black and yellow-striped Halloween costume. My competition was Ol' Gizzards, the stringy, misshapen wanker who kept falling off his bike at the start line. My competition was Comeback, the fifty-two year-old who'd had a run of Cat 3 wins back in '79 and wanted to resurrect the glories of his racing career. These were the losers I'd get to know intimately over the course of the day. The heroes of the SoCal race scene would be competition for someone else.

Our field had fifty-three riders, including Skankdaddy, a twiglike specimen doomed to flail, who bulled his way up the middle of the group, elbowing Herndy-Doo in the process. I shook my head. Why would anyone try to pass Herndy-Doo in the first minute of the race? That's like poking a bear in the balls with a sharp stick. Herndy always makes the split and he benches three-fifty.

We climbed up the first couple of miles to the right turn that led to the infamous "Punchbowl Staircase." This was a series of three climbs, each followed by a brief plateau. Like a staircase, you could see each section stretch endlessly off in front of you, and also like a staircase, it hurt like a motherfucker when you got thrown off it on your head, which is exactly what was about to happen.

By the first turn I was redlining, Comeback had gone back, Ol' Gizzards was frying in the pan, and Skankdaddy was now trying to tweezle his way across the gap between those who had been shelled and the main field. Tri-Dork looked great, which was troubling.

There were less than thirty of us left at the top of the Staircase, and we pointed our bikes down the screaming crosswind descent. After the race everyone lied about how fast we went, with the biggest whopper coming from DQ Louie, who claimed he'd hit sixty. Even so, it was a solid fifty mph for the entire five miles downhill.

I almost didn't get dropped

After the descent there was a rolling three-mile stretch before we made a sharp right and did the climb again. As the climb began I felt great. Thirty seconds in I felt not so great. Forty seconds in, the entire group detonated as G$, DQ Louie, Flagg, and Glass Hip crushed the remnants of the field, which had been reduced with the grisly awfulness of an Indonesian shrunken skull taken as a memento of war. I would have stayed with them if I hadn't gotten dropped, no question about it, and I would have attacked, too, I'm sure.

As I settled back with Gilligan, the Skipper, and the other castaways, I watched the leaders pull away. Tucked safely in their midst was Tri-Dork. All hundred and ninety pounds of him.

[Insert incredibly stupid, boring, "I"-centric recount of every dumb move, every struggle, every adjective designed to impress readers with how tough it was, every reference to grit and power and climbing and hammering for every bump, climb, descent, pull, flail, and flog of the remaining thirty-eight miles.]

At the end of the third lap we overhauled Tri-Dork, as he, Veins, and I dropped our contingent of wankers on the last time up the big climb. We hit the downhill and Tri-Dork demonstrated his mastery of the Egg. This was where he sat on the top tube, put his hands on tops of the bars, curved his spine, tucked his head, accelerated to max speed, and vaguely hoped that he didn't get clipped by a ladder dangling off a passing farm truck, or that his wheel didn't hit a pebble, or that a dog or squirrel or snake or badger or possum or rat or raccoon didn't scoot in front of him, or that the wind didn't blow him off the road, or that his tires didn't flat. When you're almost two hundred pounds it meant that you easily went fifty-five mph, which Tri-Dork did.

It also meant that his nuts were smashed flat on the top tube, a minor point, and that he lost 95% control of his bike due to the aero position. This was no problem if you were a triathlete, where blunt force trauma to the head would leave the pea-sized, cement-covered brain undamaged, but when you were a nerdy bike blogger it was a different deal and rather worrisome. All this was going through my mind as a big farm truck with a trailer full of unused IQ points flipped on its blinker and made as if to cut across our path, with Tri-Dork in full tuck, and Veins and I cowering in his draft.

Thanks to dumb luck we avoided the side of the trailer, and thanks to the Egg we caught what was left of the main field, which consisted of the saddest, tiredest, beatdownest, sad-sackest bunch of wrinkled old shits I'd ever seen. And they were the fresh ones, everyone else having quit, except for Tree, who had dropped his chain at .5 mile into the race and rode the

SETH DAVIDSON

rest of it alone.

The race for first

We found out after the race that Glass Hip, Kalashnikov, DQ Louie, Flagg, and G$ had shellacked the field at the turn onto the Stairstep on the second lap. You'd think that with three Big Orange riders represented in the group it would have been an easy win, but the Orangemen were able, just in time, to snatch defeat from the jaws of victory.

Glass Hip was on form. That meant something different than it did for most people. When he rode for the U.S. Olympic team, Glass Hip was tested along with the other elite racers. In every parameter he failed miserably. His VO2 max was 19.5 ml/kg/min. His functional threshold power was 185 watts. His torso measured twice the length of his longest leg, which was six inches longer than the other one, such that neither foot could reach the ground without a short stepladder.

However, he outscored everyone ever tested at the U.S. Olympic Center in the category of "Hammer Thumb." This was a test where they tied your hand to a board and the tester smacked your biggest digit with a ball-peen hammer. Electrodes were wired to your brain to record your ability to withstand pain, but were rarely used because after the first whack the testee usually shrieked in agony, and after the second one passed out.

They not only hammered Glass Hip's thumb,

but they hammered all his fingers and toes as well, culminating with a four-minute session on the end of his pecker. The tester finally passed out from sympathetic pain sensations, kind of like guys who go into labor when their wives give birth. When they read the computer print-out after scanning the contents of his skull, it said, "No brain detected. No brain, no pain."

Glass Hip ready to pounce

In short, no matter what they threw at him, and they threw it all, Glass Hip took it on the chin, shook it off, and braced himself for the next blow. Pretty soon, like the testers at the Olympic Training Center, his adversaries found themselves in a weakened and terrified state. As the five heroes approached the line, Glass Hip bent over, gently took the candy from the babies, and rocketed across the line effortlessly.

Baby "DQ" Louie opened up his sprunt for second place close to the gutter, then came all the way across the center line, shutting the door on Kalashnikov and earning himself yet another yellow card, relegation to fifth, and a note that he had to take home and get his mother to sign acknowledging his bad behavior.

The race for fifteenth

Tri-Dork and I, locked in mortal combat, engaged in a battle for the ages. He, doing his first road race on a course suited for small-boned anorexics, was matched against me, a tiny person who had done a thousand hilly road races. It was only by using every ounce of cunning, skill, strength, ability, tactics, and him throwing a chain at the bottom of the climb that I was able to claim the coveted spot of fifteenth place.

On the way home we re-hashed the race. "At first I thought you were bullshitting me about the hamburger and fries. But that really works. Thanks, Wankmeister."

I, for once, didn't know what to say.

SUICIDE ISN'T PAINLESS

Nor, apparently, is it easy. After swimming out into the Gulf of Mexico late at night and trying to drown himself (he swam back in because he was so afraid), then trying to asphyxiate himself with a rubber hose hooked up to the tailpipe (he went to sleep and woke up with a blinding headache), my elder brother Ian went down to the neighborhood Academy, bought a .38 nickel-plated Rossi and put a bullet in his chest.

At the funeral home they had neatly folded his hands but if you looked closely, and I always look closely, you could see the powder burns on the crease between his right thumb and forefinger. He didn't have any veins in his hands and his eyelids sank unnaturally into his head. He'd donated his eyes and everything else of salvage value to people who needed it more than he did, which, at this point, was everyone. The sleeves in his suit were completely flat and looked empty but I didn't have the nerve to ask the funeral director what had happened to his arms.

They'd tried to cut and stretch and twist his face back into something that might have looked like Ian. It reminded me of the time I'd tried to throw clay on a wheel. Once it gets out of shape you can't ever put it back into shape. It's all fucked up forever.

This weird cosmetic mess of flesh and

chemicals and clothes was all that was left of my brother, a terrible visual legacy so vivid that it still overcomes a lifetime of other memories.

Let me count the ways

Suicide is apparently painful in the planning. It's painful in the execution. And it's painful in the aftermath. The pain ripples out, not like a poetic pebble tossed into a reflecting pool, but like a massive, horrible, endless discharge of vomit with your head hung over the toilet, splattering and splashing and staining and stinking and ruining everything it touches. And it touches everything.

Suicide's painful in the telling. For some it's an embarrassment. For me it's painful because Ian's not the first person in the world to kill himself, and as I say it my friends and acquaintances share the spatter in their own lives with me. The sister hanged herself. The father shot himself on the son's eighteenth birthday. The goddaughter did herself in after a happy, normal phone call. The brother threw himself off the balcony. Ian's choice, for someone so imaginative and creative and original, was so pedestrian. It was another suicide, one more bloody horrific mess that family got to find and strangers in hazmat suits had to clean up. For a fee.

Suicide is unquestionably painful in the discovering. Dad checked his email at 8:00 AM on Saturday, June 16, Central Standard Time, conveniently before Father's Day. Three emails sat percolating in his inbox, all from Ian, all time-stamped at 7:03 that morning. "Tired of living. By the time you read this I'll be dead." Etcetera.

Suicide is unbearably painful in the confirming. Screeching through traffic, blowing through red lights, frantically dashing up the rickety staircase and bursting into the filthy and debris-strewn apartment to find your eldest slumped over on the couch, the ragged drainage hole from the .38 having emptied the contents of Ian's heart onto the sofa, and the dead fact of death leaving Dad there with his firstborn, deadened.

For whom the bell tolls

Suicide is painful in the alerting. I'd just finished up a Donut Ride beatdown, and it's odd how good I felt after such an abject thrashing. Shredded on the Switchbacks, unceremoniously dumped in Better Homes, shelled on the way up to the Domes, caught and dropped after the Glass Church sprint, and DFL all the way up Zumaya, what right did I have to feel good? I dunno, but I felt good.

"Seth?" Dad said over the phone and he didn't have to say anything else because I knew it was bad. A few hours later I was on a plane to Houston.

Suicide is unbearably painful in the sharing. I didn't want to go over to the apartment and find out how we were going to clean up the mess, but someone had to. That couch looked at me with an evil sneer, its cushions spotted with unthinkably huge circles of gore where Ian had slumped, blood gushing out of the hole, the back of the couch decorated with an enormous, thick clot that looked like a giant painter with a giant paint knife had cut out the biggest chunk of red oil off the palette and smeared it on the fabric, a clump bigger and thicker than five fists stuck to the couch and thinning towards the bottom into a pooled spill.

To think: All that raggedy, jagged exit wound, mess and destruction caused by the same thing that made the small, neat, perfectly round hole in the wall where the bullet had passed into the next apartment. "What a fucking idiot," I though. "He could have killed his fucking neighbor."

Suicide makes you angry, too.

I stared at the awfulness wishing I had a delete button, but it's been recorded permanently on my soft drive. The biohazard disposal contractor dude smoking a cigarette and driving a big white van that said "Plumbers" on the side next to a hand-lettered "Bio-Expert Cleaners" was humane and human.

"Sorry for your loss, man," he said in the ninety degree heat and stifling humidity as we stood outside the apartment.

"Yeah," I said. Me, too."

Nothing ends like it's supposed to

Suicide's painful because it blames you. Unlike the cancer or the runaway truck or the accidental drowning, suicide's uniquely the fault of the survivors. What could I have done differently? Was it something I said or did? Why didn't I see the signs? Where was I when he needed me most? Oh yeah, I remember. I was on the Donut Ride, pedaling my bike while he was bleeding out on the couch. Natch.

Suicide's painful because Ian's the person responsible for my decision in 1982 to buy a road bike. The person who inspired the gift that has made me happiest was so terribly unhappy that he killed himself. The word for that is "irony."

Of course nothing is all bad. Despite this ghastly ordeal, there's something good and positive that has come out of it. But I'll be dogdamned if I know what it is.

The longest ride

Back in Los Angeles I showed up on Tuesday to find that the NPR that day was dedicated to my brother. Slightly more than seventy people rolled out from the Manhattan Beach Pier at 6:40 AM. By the time we turned onto Westchester Parkway the peloton was easily a hundred strong.

Christine Reilly, Stella Tong, Greg Leibert, Lauren Mulwitz, Joe Yule, Vickie VanOs Castaldi, Izzie VanOs Castaldi, Chris Gregory, Kristabel, Suze Sonye, Jay Yoshizumi, Brian Perkins, Gus Bayle, Rahsaan Bahati, Cary Alpert, Sarah Mattes, Greg Seyranian, Dara Richman, and David Perez made the plan and got the word out so that people were at the

Pier well in advance of the start time. Vickie and Greg took the sixty-five handmade armbands, beautifully lettered by Izzie with "R.I.P. Ian, '62-'12" and tied one to each person's arm. Then Dave Kramer introduced Greg, who made a short, moving, and beautiful speech about my brother, someone he had never met but someone who, through me, he felt like he knew.

I clipped in and led us out onto the bike path. Then I pulled off and floated to the back, where I was overcome by the sight of the yellow armbands fluttering in the breeze. My friends, as well as people I'd never even met, had done this for me. Emily and Chris had come over from the west side just to be there. Others who couldn't make it like Dara and Laurie were there in spirit, and still others showed up at TELO in the evening and shared their sympathies and condolences. I'll never be able to repay any of them.

It's a very good debt to owe, and to owe forever.

Girls and bikes

I got into cycling as a result of my brother, indirectly. His second year of high school he got in a horrific fight with my mom about the car. Our parents had divorced a couple of years before, and it was the kind of hateful, acrimonious, bitter divorce that paralyzes the kids and poisons your life for the next few decades, like battery acid in the ice cream. Ian was tired of fighting over the car and one day he went out and bought a black Fuji touring bike. It cost two hundred bucks, an incomprehensible amount of money, and it was an act of complete rebellion, as the bicycle so often is.

Going from a Jeep Cherokee Golden Eagle to a bicycle? I had one conclusion: "Dork." At the same time I was thrilled that I no longer had to fight with him for Cherokee privileges. He got the dorkmobike, I got the uberwagon.

Within a couple of weeks I discovered the source of his inspiration. His girlfriend was a cyclist and they biked everywhere together. "He's still a dork," I thought.

Then a couple of weeks after that I began to hear moaning and groaning coming out of his bedroom. This was way before Internet porn. It was awesome, and he was a dork no more. "What a stud!" I thought. "That bike deal is pretty cool!"

Buses and bikes

Although I didn't rush out and get a bike to aid in the quick dispatch of my virginity, the idea remained that bikes, which I now associated with sex, were cool. This was partly because Ian had let me test ride his Fuji a few times and it was so different from the rusted out Murray that I'd used for three years to commute to Jane Long Junior High that it hardly felt like a bicycle.

My freshman year in college at the University of Texas, 1982, my parents refused to let me have a car. My antics in high school convinced them a car would prematurely end my college career, and possibly my life. I lived in the Village Glen Apartments out on Burton, six or seven miles from campus, and had to take the shuttle bus, which in those days was run by union-busting Laidlaw. They employed hippie stoners from the 60's and 70's to drive the buses and paid just enough to keep the hippies in weed, ensuring that there would never be any unionizing.

"Let's fuckin' organize, dude."

Pfffffffffffffffff. "Later."

The Village Glen was one of the last bus stops on the Riverside Route before getting on I-35 and going to campus, so in the morning the buses were always full. That meant having to get to the bus stop early, as the first bus or two rarely had room for even one more passenger. One morning in October I was standing in the rain waiting for the bus. The first one passed me and splashed me. The second one passed me. The third one roared by with an "Out of Service" sign on the front.

I screamed at the driver and flipped him off. He braked. I'd never seen a whole bus go sideways. Out bounded the raging hippie, fists balled and murder in his eyes. If I hadn't been so weak-looking and petrified he would have killed me. Instead he screamed. "How about I beat you into a fucking pulp you snotnosed little fuck?" he roared.

"Uh, I, I, I'm really sorry. Please don't hit me!"

I begged.

"You ever fucking give me any attitude on a bus I'm driving I'll break you in half you little prick. They don't pay me enough in this shit job to put up with bullshit from spoiled little assholes like you!"

"Yes, sir," I mumbled. "I'm really sorry."

[To crack dealer] "So, should I start using crack?"

I had to wait another twenty minutes in the cold, pelting rain. During those twenty minutes I went from being grateful that I'd get to school with all of my teeth to angry at being a bus sheep. My resentment built throughout morning classes and exploded in an epiphany when my last course finished at noon. "I'm gonna buy a bike just like my brother did! Screw Laidlaw! Screw that hippie stoner fucker! Screw the rain!"

It was the bicycle, again revolutionizing someone's mind and shortly thereafter his life.

I practically ran down 24th Street to Freewheeling Bicycles and Crackhouse, where I realized something else after walking the aisle and looking at the shiny, beautiful bicycles. "Wow, I'm broke!"

Fortunately, Uncle Phil Tomlin had just the bike for me, a Nishiki International with Suntour derailleurs, Dia Compe brakes, and Sugino cranks. At a paltry $375.00, I'd be able to easily afford it as long as I didn't eat in November. Food or bike? It was an easy choice, especially with Uncle Phil kindly and professionally assisting me with my first crack purchase.

From then on I became a bike junkie, and a year later I'd already been voted "Most Likely to be Run Over by a Car" by my riding buddies. 1984 was my breakout year, when I dominated the Bloor Road to Blue Bluff Time Trial and won a coveted Laverne and Shirley board game for first place. The thirty-plus years after buying that first bike have flown by, and somehow I was still riding with the same yippee as the day I pedaled that Nishiki out of the Freewheeling parking lot.

This is gonna hurt me and it's gonna hurt you

So this thing that has given me so much joy, this thing that has surrounded me with friends who are often closer than family, is a gift from my brother. I thought about that while Greg spoke. He paid me the ultimate compliment in the process, saying that they had come to honor my brother because without him, I wouldn't be part of their community.

There's no other way to say this than to say I felt more loved than I have ever felt in my life. Sweaty, muscled men threw their arms around me and sweaty, muscled, beautiful women did, too, each one saying something that sounded like love, regardless of the words. And as proof that these weren't just empty phrases, when we hit the bottom of Pershing they went so hard so fast that I was almost blinded by the pain.

"This one," Jaeger said as he came by with the ferocity of a jungle beast, "is for Ian."

There's a place for gentleness and for camaraderie. It's called the bricks on the Manhattan Beach Starbucks after the ride. The NPR itself is a place for the unbridled beatdown, relentless attacking into the wind, and the crushing of the weak by the strong.

"Should we do a memorial lap in silence?"

"Fuck that, dude."

"Give Wankmeister the win?"

"He wouldn't want it and I wouldn't give it."

Suffice it to say that that day I was the weak and others were the strong, and the law of the jungle prevailed, as it always did. But even though I was weak and struggled at the end, I didn't get crushed. I got carried along by the unlikeliest thing of all, a raft of soft yellow ribbons floating in the breeze.

LANCE 3.0: LAY DOWN YOUR CUDGELS, PLEASE

Newsflash: Lance Armstrong has been stripped of pretty much everything.

Tour titles? Gone.

Reputation? Gone.

Income stream from his cancer foundation? Gone.

Ability to compete in sanctioned athletic events and the attendant income? Gone.

Mansion in Austin? Gone (but replaced with a cooler one).

Self-respect after not getting hugged by Oprah? Totally gone.

Bonus newsflash: It's not over yet. The Justice Department has joined Floyd Landis's whistleblower suit, former sponsors are suing to get their money back, and a class action lawsuit has been filed for alleged false claims made regarding FRS energy drink. Lance will be paying for his transgressions for a long, long time.

I don't know about you...

But I believe in redemption. Not the Shawshank kind; I believe in the kind of redemption that says once you've been punished for your transgressions according to rule and/or law, you're redeemed.

This type of redemption may not mean that you're a sterling moral character or even that you admit guilt or feel sorry for what you've done. It means that you broke the rule, got punished, and are now free to move on. Something worthless has been exchanged for something useful and new, just like a coupon.

When you murder someone, rape someone, abuse a child, defraud the elderly, skim from the company till, or run a red light, your redemption begins when you've served your time or paid your fine. Redemption means trading in the old for the new. It means a fresh start. And in case you were wondering, along with the punishment fitting the crime, redemption is the premise upon which our entire legal system is built.

Redemption gives convicted felons the right to vote, the right to work, the right to have a passport, and the right to fully participate as citizens once they've served their time. Redemption doesn't mean you have to like the sinner or the ex-con, but it does mean you can't legally continue punishing and persecuting him.

Lance is no convicted felon. If you don't think he's been punished, see above. If you're still harboring resentment and anger, that's understandable. But he's not going anywhere, and I'd suggest that there's a better way to deal with him than continually bludgeoning him for his transgressions.

It's an old concept, actually. It's called forgiveness.

Cranking up the PR machine

Lance has begun doing what he does best, going on the offensive. Whether it's calling Patrick Brady and chatting with him for an hour or unblocking Lesli Cohen and a bunch of other diehard Lance opponents on Twitter, it's clear that he has a plan in place and has begun to execute it.

What's the plan?

The plan is to get back in front of the sports media and build Lance 3.0. This newest iteration is simple. Lance 3.0 is a —

1. Survivor.
2. Family man.
3. World class athlete.
4. Wiser man.
5. Friend.

What will Lance 3.0 do? He will sell something. What will he sell? I don't know. But I do know this. He won't be setting up a pyramid scheme to defraud Medicare or a criminal syndicate to assassinate journalists. Possibly, he's got a plan that will let him earn a living as a speaker/athlete/patient advocate.

Is that so bad? How many other people get

out of prison and see their mission in life as one dedicated to helping others? I don't know that that's his plan, but what does he have left? And why is it contemptible for him to try and rebuild a career that's been destroyed through his own mistakes?

Ultimately, though, does it really matter what his end game is? No.

What matters is you

A group of local riders were climbing Latigo Canyon Road the other day, and guess who they met at the top? Barry Bonds.

Remember him?

He's the guy who was held up as one of the most evil and crooked baseball players of all time, the guy who stole Hank Aaron's home run record on the strength of drugs and lies. Today he's a slim and fit bicycle rider.

When the gang ran into him on Latigo no one cringed, or cursed him, or called him a scumbag doper. Instead, they mugged for the camera and posted photos on Facebook.

Why?

First, of course, is star power, and we are here in L.A. Second is the fact that Barry has paid for what he did, and he didn't even go on Oprah and confess. We know that he was caught, that he's been punished, and that now he's just a dude on a bike who used to hit a lot of home runs with the help of a lot of drugs. We also know a lot of his contemporaries did the same thing and got off scot-free. Our lives should be too short to keep hating a guy who's been punished to the full extent that the system demanded, particularly since all he seems to do now is pedal around, show up at the occasional crit and act like a normal dude.

We're done with his crime, and so is he. Now we just want to say hello, snap a pic, and ride our bikes.

What about Lance?

Lance is different from Barry because the latter earned hundreds of millions of dollars and wisely invested them over the course of a long career. Barry doesn't have to work.

Lance has five kids, huge ongoing legal bills, and a lot of years left to live. It's impossible that he's got anywhere near the pile that Barry is sitting on, or even anything close to it. Unlike Barry, Lance has to work. Rather than pulling up the drawbridge and living inside the fort, Lance has got to get out and mingle in order to rebuild.

For people getting out of prison and living in halfway houses, it's called "You have to get a job." We encourage convicted rapists, killers, and swindlers to get out and make an honest buck after they've done their time.

Lance showed us that pro cycling is a corrupt freak show. Danilo di Luca confirmed that it still is in the 2013 Giro. Critics say that Nibali, Wiggins, Dave

Brailsford, Chris Froome, Pat McQuaid, Hein Verbruggen, and USA Cycling are reaffirmation that anyone who thinks the sport is clean isn't thinking very hard. At the local level in California, systematic drug testing is being instituted for masters racers as of 2013. You know, "masters," the elderly people who race bikes as a hobby and who apparently have so completely emulated their pro heroes that they've taken to drugs and, still unsatisfied, will now experience the ultimate in verisimilitude by getting tested as well.

If you hate Lance because he "ruined the sport," maybe it's time YOU moved on. The pro sport is rotten and has always been rotten. If you follow it and still bury your head in the jocks of its stars there's a problem all right, and the problem is with you. If you can watch Nibali repeatedly hit the gas in the snow at the end of the most grueling stage of the most grueling race while his competition is rolling over and dying on the slopes, you're the one who needs to analyze my modification of this old saw: "Fool me once, shame on you, fool me twice, shame on me. Fool me over and over and over, and I'm watching a bike race."

As Billy Stone might put it, "And the dopers ruined your life as a Cat 4 masters athlete exactly how?"

Where's it all going?

Now that Lance 1.0 and 2.0 have been

airbrushed out of the history books — a monstrously bizarre step since other busted and confessed dopers have not been — what's wrong with giving Lance 3.0 the same degree of redemption that should be afforded to axe murderers, tax cheats, misdemeanor DUI's, and kids on grade probation in college? How is our agenda advanced by refusing to lay down arms, and instead insisting that he be treated like the unrepentant, unpunished cheat that he was a year ago, when he's repented and been punished?

Does it ennoble us to keep shrieking "Off with his head!" after his head has been offed, stuck on a pike, and paraded around his kids' schoolyards? I think it does the opposite. It shows us up to be petty, vengeful creeps who actually think that pro cycling is so important it transcends common notions of justice and fair play.

Five years hence, ten years hence, Lance 3.0 will have been fully rebuilt. He's that smart, he's that hard working, and he's that motivated. He's also got close to four million people on Twitter who want to know what he says and thinks as well as five kids to feed, clothe, and put through college.

In other words, he's not going anywhere. Do you want to be the wild-eyed crazy standing on the street corner screaming, "He doped! He cheated! He lied! He ruined my Cat 4 masters racing career!"

I don't.

If the UCI and USA Cycling and WADA are done with his case then I am, too. Keep clubbing at him if you want, but don't expect me to join in. I'd rather go club some of the baby seals on next Tuesday's NPR.

SHE WASN'T A CYCLIST.
SHE WAS A PERSON.

Suzanne Rivera is dead. Contrary to comments posted in various news articles, she didn't die doing what she loved. She died trying to avoid a race support van that had parked in the middle of a fast, blind, downhill curve, obstructing part of the lane for no good reason at all.

Presumably, her last thoughts were "Oh my God, I'm going to hit the back of that van!" Presumably, she was frightened. I'd go so far as to say she was terrified beyond belief, like every other cyclist in the history of two wheels who, in that split second between realization and impact, knows that this may well be the last thing she ever sees.

No, she didn't die doing what she loved. And no, it wasn't unavoidable. And no, the fact that she was a brand new racer with brand new bike handling skills can't be ruled out as a factor in her death.

I'm not blaming anybody

This isn't a blame game. I am, however, pointing out the horror and revulsion and senselessness and loss we feel when someone dies or suffers a catastrophic injury riding a bike. We feel it because it feels an awful lot like us. Whether Jorge

Alvarado on a training ride, Robert Hyndman on a challenging descent, or Suzanne Rivera in a twisty road race, these deaths shake us to our core, and they should. They must.

The dead are young men with their entire lives ahead of them. They are mothers acting as role models for their young children by practicing fitness and engaging in a healthy activity. They are retirees finding pastimes that are social and fun. They are us, and their deaths remind us that when you roll out the door, happy and excited and anticipating the yippee that awaits, there is a reasonable chance that you might not return, ever.

In Suzanne's case the horror and tragedy are compounded by something else known as the unspoken rule of the road. Coming hard on the heels of a hospital visit last week where I saw a cyclist and wonderful friend in the earliest stages of recovery from a broken neck, it has occurred to me that we must not let the rule, the secret rule, go unspoken any longer.

We have a duty to remind people of it, especially the beginners, and even more especially the beginners who decide to pin on a number and lock horns. We have a duty to tell this secret rule because it is a dirty one, a painful one, and also a hard truth, and it is this: If you're going to ride fast, you are going to crash.

And the rule has a corollary almost as terrible as the secret itself: You will crash not once, but many times and the chances are fair that at least one of your crashes will leave you with a broken bone or an injury to your head or spine.

Would you still ride if you knew?

If, before purchasing that brand new bike, you were to read a list of the injured and a description of their injuries just from the people who regularly do the local Donut Ride, would you still decide that this is the sport for you? Some would.

If, before entering your first mass start event, you were to read a list of the people who'd been hospitalized after going down in a bike race in the last twelve months, would you still pin on the number? Some people would.

Why?

Because for a lot of people, the life they're in pursuit of isn't a life of comfort and safety and freedom from risk.

A beautiful life

After reading the news accounts, statements by her friends and teammates, and her obituary, one thing is clear. Suzanne Rivera lived a beautiful life. Surely she appreciated the risks of racing a bike. The waiver she signed says you can get seriously injured or killed. Everyone reads it. Everyone thinks about it, however briefly, before deciding that it probably won't happen to them. Everyone signs it.

Yet even more surely, she appreciated the feelings of power and strength and competition that are unique to bike racing. Her life seemed to be about her husband, her children, and taking the challenging path rather than the safe one. When the gauntlet was thrown down, she picked it up at an age when most people are trying to find the easy groove, not test themselves against the relentlessness of the road.

Those of us who continue to push hard, knowing what may follow, are following in her footsteps.

Why?

For me, and probably for you, it's because we know no other path.

With the hardness of marathons in her legs and the steel bit of the bike between her teeth, it was the only path that Suzanne knew, too. May her newfound serenity be a worthy end to such a long, hard, beautiful road.

HARD MAN'S COOKIES

New Girl's eyes flexed open at 5:00 AM, beating her alarm clock to the punch by half an hour. A smile crept over her face.

She swung her legs over the edge of the bed and reached for the elastic band on her nightstand, quickly tying her hair into a ponytail. She pulled the ponytail tight and smiled again.

Her clothes were neatly laid out on the cedar chest at the foot of the bed. She'd chosen bib shorts, jersey, and arm warmers that all said "Donut Ride," and not just because it was the Donut Ride, and not just because it was her favorite kit, and not just because Junkyard, who'd designed it, would be riding with her. She had also chosen it because rain was already lightly beating down outside her bedroom window, and she'd learned the hard way not to wear white kits on rainy days.

She smiled again.

In a few minutes the oatmeal was bubbling on the stove. It had that roasted smell, like coffee, but more wholesome, creamy and foaming and bubbling on the top. She loved to watch it swirl and make patterns, but most of all she loved to laugh at it, because oatmeal was so funny.

Here she was, starting each and every day with oatmeal, even though she'd gone out of her way to poke fun at Wankmeister's FB posts that regularly featured images of gray-as-death oatmeal with raisins bubbling in the top like rabbit pellets. Oatmeal was funny, she decided again, and smiled at the pan. It foamed and bubbled in a way that, if you cocked your head right, looked kind of like it was smiling back at you.

The meeting place

New Girl kitted up and pulled on her clear plastic rain cape. She'd spent thirty minutes in the bike shop picking a rain cape, and went with this one because even though it wasn't very snazzy, it was clear, and clear was what she wanted so that the Donut Ride logo would show through, even in the rain.

She went into the garage and ran a cloth over Princess. She'd cleaned it the night before, and she smiled at the sparkling cogs and well oiled chain. "Enough to wet it, not drown it," Junkyard had told her. It sparkled, just in time to get covered with muck and filth and grime and fun, especially covered with fun.

She rolled out of the garage, each foot clicking with that life-affirming lock of pedal to cleat, binding her to the machine, making them one. Now the decisions she made were binding. Now whatever happened to Princess would also happen to her.

The simple rain beat harder against her but inside her three skins she was dry and warm and smiling at the shiny, muffled world. The thought of meeting her mates made her push just a little harder. As she came up the slight bump, eagerly looking into the parking lot at Catalina Coffee, her smile fell. The lot was empty.

Calling in sick

New Girl got off her bike and stood under the concrete arch. She looked at her phone. Tumbleweed and Madeline, who lived around the corner, had texted the night before to say they were opting for less rain and more bed. New Girl had smiled again and texted back, "OK! I'll be at CC and pedaling anyway! HAGD!"

She sat back to wait, realizing that she was early, as usual. Very early, as usual.

After a long while her first surprise came when Tumbleweed and Madeline appeared. "Not going to let you ride alone!" said Madeline.

Then Gussy appeared from out of the light rainy fog, his jersey halfway unzipped and carpets of wet chest hair spilling out. He was already smirking. "You can call me 'Gorilla in the Mist,'" he said, and everyone laughed.

As the other riders appeared, Gussy's monologue of jokes, tales from the old days, observations on Krispy Kreme, and predictions about how the Donut Ride beatdown would unfold kept everyone grinning. But New Girl grinned biggest because she was smiling on the inside as well.

With Toronto and Junkyard in formation they all rolled out for a pre-loop, destined to get them to the start of the Donut with just enough time for coffee and a bathroom break.

Warming up for a beatdown

New Girl loved the pre-loop best of all, even in the rain when the road was shiny and trying hard to jerk her wheels out from under her. The road striping, the Botts dots, the oily runoff, the slick leaves and fallen pine cones and magnolia cones all conspired to knock her over, but she smiled her way through it, so happy to be pushing up the little kicker by the golf course that she forgot to talk or chat or do anything other than grin.

Now they were soaked and back at the Riviera Village for the final call-up before the massacre. New Girl wheeled up to the Coffee Bean and Tea Leaf and smiled some more as she saw more of her buddies. There's the Pilot; there's the Bull; there's Arkansas Traveler; there's Sparkles; and oh! Look! Over in the corner looking all sour and out of sorts but really not sour or out of sorts at all, it's Wankmeister! She smiled big, and he smiled back in his finest Donut morning scowl.

The group pushed out, the rain stopped, and fifty or so riders filled out the peloton. New Girl smiled at Suze, at G$, at Dawg, at Motorhead, and at Prez! She thought she might run out of smiles before they hit the first climb out of Malaga Cove, but she didn't.

New Girl didn't know it in words but this was the secret of the congregants of the Church of the Spinning Wheel. The faces and backs and bikes and legs are as familiar to you as you are to them, and with familiarity comes trust and with trust the elemental core of us rises to the surface, our humanity, in other words our belonging to and our place in the tribe.

Legs to brain: We're not part of the tribe anymore

Up the climb out of Malaga Cove, New Girl felt the sting and then the throb and then the fire in her lungs. She wasn't smiling anymore as she locked onto the wheel in front of her, praying she'd make it over the climb with the group, hoping that her ride wouldn't end here as it sometimes did, before it had even properly started.

A split second of inattention and she wobbled, smacking into Junkyard who was alongside her. He gave her a friendly smile but she was terrified. She'd almost knocked down her best buddy, what was she doing here, she was redlining, she was a hazard to the group, the road was incredibly slick and it had started raining again.

She'd been kicked out the back so hard the week before that by the time she reached Hawthorne, alone, she'd had to pull over into the parking lot of the 7-11 and sob, and now here she was again about to get her ticket punched. At the moment of disconnecting, a rider who'd been watching the whole mini-drama reached over and gave her a hard push that was gloved in five words of encouragement and faith. "You can do it, dig." She'd never even seen him before.

She dug as hard as she ever had, hanging on by a thread until she was over the bump. She caught her breath as the sucking of the peloton dragged her through Paseo del Mar, along the bluffs and the million-dollar mansions with the billion-dollar views that the congregants of the Church of the Spinning Wheel all got to enjoy for the price of a bike and some pain, until she found herself on Pilot's wheel. The next big acceleration came through Lunada Bay, and this time the kick was hard and sharp and it piled on top of the several jumps already withdrawn from her account which meant it was every man and woman for herself, and so New Girl came unhitched and was off the back.

She was smiling, though because she'd made it longer than the week before, and when a couple of riders came by they rode a steady paceline up to Trump National, the gateway to the Switchbacks. At the slight rise the riders left her and she was by herself again.

As she gathered herself for the big push, New Girl felt her rear tire go soft, then flat. The rain had started up again. The group atop the Switchbacks wouldn't know she'd flatted and they'd continue on. For the first time that morning, her inside smile frowned.

If you have to grow up, be like the Fireman

A handful of people in the South Bay are larger than life. The Fireman is one of them. He looks gruff and road-hardened and ready to take whatever you can dish out and still pay you back double, then drink you under the table plus beat you in the sprint or give you the lead-out from hell that you'll remember for the rest of your life if you ever manage to come around it, but it doesn't take anything at all to get underneath the callused exterior and find a heart as large and kind and generous as any, anywhere.

Maybe it's because his day job involves roadside visits to catastrophic freeway collisions, or because his night job takes him to blazing infernos venting poisonous gas and smoke and death, or because his summer holidays take him to raging wildfires throughout L.A. County, maybe that's what explains him, but I think there's more to it than that. I think there's something of the man, the husband, the father, the patriarch who opens his door to friends and feeds them from his table until they can eat no more and swallow not another single drop, this is what explains him, he is a throwback to the days of the tribe, he would have been the leader of the clan, the first one to throw the spear or lead the charge or repulse the invading horde, the first one to christen the infant or bless the newly-wedded couple or mark the conquered ground as hallowed, it's this, his Stone Age mantle of hunter, gatherer, and leader of the tribe that makes him what he is, the one we all look up to without knowing why.

Which is a fancy, long-ass way of saying he stopped to help New Girl change her flat and change it in a flat fucking jiffy.

Then he paced her up the Switchbacks to a new Strava record.

Then he continued on his way after perfecting her day and restoring her smile before she could even say "Thanks."

Mud stockings

New Girl got home from the Donut Ride, legs covered in mud, and after cleaning up she got to work.

An hour and a half later she was knocking on the firehouse door. A burly fireman answered. "Yes?"

"Here," she said. "These are for you guys."

"Oh," said the fireman. "Is it something we said?"

She laughed. "It's something you DID, silly."

"You gonna let me in on the secret?"

"No," she said with the biggest of smiles. "But it involves a flat bicycle tire."

The firehouse dude smiled big, too, the circle now complete.

LETTER TO A LITTLE KID

When you grow up you're going to ask about your father. You're going to ask how he died. You're going to feel the wordless pain of going through life without your dad. You're never going to have the guy who gave you half your blood, half your genes, and all of your heart standing next to you at those moments in life when you most desperately need a father. Little kid, you've lost half of the most important thing any kid can ever have before your life has even begun.

Your dad died racing his bike in an amateur weekend crit. And you want to know why, and no one's been able to explain. How can anyone explain something as senseless and pointless as dying in a weekend bike race, chasing the glory of a candy bar prime and twenty-five bucks in prize money?

Why we race

Before I try to explain why he died, let me try to explain what he was doing when he died. Your dad, who had been racing his bike for years, was taking a life or death risk and he knew it. He even signed a piece of paper that said he knew the risk was so big it might kill him.

But here's the thing, little kid: He knew it, but he didn't really believe it. If he had known, or had any idea that getting killed in that bike race might actually happen to him and leave you behind without your dad, he would have never been in that race. He wanted you and your mom at that race so you could watch him compete and maybe even win. You were only a couple of years old, but you were so excited by the race and seeing your dad in it that even after he crashed, each time the pack came around you pointed at the peloton and said "Daddy! Daddy!" It was so cute, before we found out that your dad had died. After that it was heartbreaking.

Your dad was well known and respected in his bicycling community. He raced his bike for the same reason we all race our bikes. We want to see how good we are compared to the other people that day, that time, that event, when we stick the safety pins into our numbers and mass at the start line to find out how much we can endure, to battle with our friends without fighting them, and in some sense to put everything on the line.

Everything.

Why you were at that race, little kid

If we just looked at that bike race and at what you've lost, there's no way it was worth it. No hobby is worth dying for. No little kid deserves to lose his dad like that.

But it wasn't just a hobby, little kid. These people who were around him when he died, they were his friends. They were the people who helped him when he flatted, they were the people he helped when it was they who had a mechanical. They were the people he laughed with, the people he suffered with, and the people he joined at day's end to sit down and share a beer with.

Little kid, living in a community, whether you're lucky enough to have a community of friends, a community of family, or both, is the only thing that makes life worth living. Without people around you to love, to share the good, to help fend off the bad, and to laugh at the absurd, we're not living. That loneliness of not having a community of friends can kill people, little kid, just as surely as hitting a utility pole killed your dad. It's the loneliness that took the life of someone I loved, too.

But your dad, he lived. And when he entered the world of bike racing he entered the world of a bleeding, life or death intensity that those who haven't done it can never understand. It's a world of fear, of loathing, of pain, of exhilaration, of speed, of triumph, of defeat, and of unmitigated battle. It doesn't make you better, or smarter, or even happier, but while you're doing it you're as completely, intensely, and thoroughly alive as anything else you'll ever do, living so that your mind and body expand to fill the entirety of the time and space you occupy. You become, so briefly, the moment itself. When it's done, you can only vaguely believe that the person who did it was really you.

That was your dad's world, and the people he

did it with were his people. What's hardest to understand, little kid, is that in our bike racing community we're friends with people we've never even met. And I'll try to explain that part, too.

Passing the torch

Your dad loved you more than you'll ever know. How do I know? Because I'm a dad. Dads love their sons deeply and profoundly and wildly and also with the recognition that the little kid is going to be a man someday, and the man that the little kid becomes will outstrip the dad. It's pride and love and expectation and respect and even a little chagrin, all mixed into one.

Your dad loved you so much that he wanted you to be part of his community. You would have grown up around bikes and bike racers and you would have learned some lessons, lessons like "The correct number of bikes to own is n +1, where 'n' equals your current number of bikes." Lessons like "Beer goes with bikes, but don't overdo it."

You would have learned other things too, crucial ingredients that go into the recipe of making a little kid into a man.

"There is no 'try.'"
"Give it everything you've got."
"Overcome your fear."
"Don't give up."
"Help your friends."
"Take big risks."

And the biggest one of all? "Teach by example."

That's the biggest one of all little kid, because through his community and his hobby your dad was setting you up to learn all those lessons. He was setting you up to learn about adversity, about good times, about doing your best, about taking big risks, and about friendship. So when you ask why your dad had to die doing a weekend crit, there's part of your answer. He loved you and knew no other way to teach than through example.

Whether you ride bikes or race them when you get older doesn't matter. What matters is that you know how much he loved you and how much he wanted you to learn those life lessons that every boy has to learn in order to make his way as a man.

The wheels around you

After your dad died it created an earthquake of shock in his bicycle riding community. People who knew him and people who didn't immediately thought of you, little kid. We thought about you because some of us have little kids too, little kids who clap and cheer in between soda pops on race day. But those of us without kids had you uppermost in our minds, too. We love you too, little kid, even though we don't know you.

We love you because what happened to your dad could have happened to any one of us, and we know it. We felt the awfulness this way — "That could have been me." — and because we're part of your dad's community and therefore yours, we want you to know that you'll never be alone.

We can't replace your dad or even come close. But your dad's life will be memorialized and he'll have left behind something for you that's worth more than any insurance policy: A legacy and reputation in his community, a community of friends who won't ever forget him, and a community of friends who will be there for you if grow up and decide to follow where he led.

Peace out for now, little kid. We've got your back.

WHAT I SAW ON YOUR FACE WHEN YOU THOUGHT NO ONE WAS LOOKING

There's a gentle beauty that pours forth from your face when you're turning the pedals,

A happiness that is so warm and engulfing that it beckons us all, smilingly,

To throw off the leaden suits and ties and business blouses of our daily grind,

A happiness accompanied by a vaguely risqué nod that telegraphs an invitation to skinny-dip

In the alluring, sometimes cool, sometimes fiery hot, always rewarding pool of lycra and rubber

And carbon and shiny mirrored lenses hiding laughter and truth not even for a second,

Of flexing thighs and straining calves and beautiful sweating muscles that are driving us onward to the summit,

Or plunging us with our hearts in our throats at a million miles an hour through woods and rocks and ravines and ocean overlooks,

Or just easily rolling through the wind, the sun, and the hurting blue sky or the gently bucking pavement of the Parkway,

Knotted to one another and to the surging
throng of bodies
As each of us shares and explores and pushes
that invisible envelope binding us together,
Even as we strain with bursting chests to
bend beyond the speeding world's edge
And fly, faster, alone.

YOU'D BETTER ENJOY THE RIDE

Robert Eugene Hyndman left this world on the morning of Saturday, November 5, 2011 courtesy of a powerful blow to the head. The slight rubber strips only a few millimeters wide that anchored his bike to the surface of the road and that therefore anchored him to the world of the living, lost traction with the pavement. He was flung headlong into a metal guardwire, airlifted to the hospital, and died of his injuries.

Just.

Like.

That.

Everyone familiar with the treacherous, technical, terrifying descent that is Las Flores Canyon thought the same thing and we thought it in unison. "Could have been me."

But you know what? It wasn't.

Why?

Hearsay comes first

If the life and death of Robert Hyndman were to hold any interest for you, you'd have needed to take a moment to read the links to news reports and cycling blogs that reported his death. They were instructive, they were moving, and they formed the basis for what I'm about to write, which may not be comforting if the rough, rusty edge of reality frightens you as it does me.

None of the news reports or blog reports discussed the thing that every cyclist wants to know when they hear of a fatality, i.e. "How did it happen?"

Hyndman's accident was variously described as "veering onto the wrong side of the road," "losing control," and "hitting a guardrail." We know those are bullshit explanations because they explain nothing. Riders don't veer into the oncoming traffic lane on a fast descent unless something goes wrong. Cyclists don't lose control unless some unexpected event disrupts them. What happened?

No one saw the crash. In a conversation with one of the people who was on the ride, the closest I got to an explanation of what happened was this. Hyndman had gone into a previous turn too hot and was cautioned by his brother, an experienced rider who had been cycling for thirty years. Although he wasn't going particularly fast, as he rounded the next turn he locked the brakes and shot straight into the guardwire. He struck head first. There was, according to another person with whom I spoke, no equipment failure, just a fast moving bike, a turn, and a guardrail comprised of taut wires stretched between posts.

This scenario in which the facts were so minimal was problematic because without them all we were really doing was opining. But if the above account really is what happened, then we had a scenario, and therefore it became possible to do the unpleasant job of filling in that scenario with people, decisions, and consequences.

What is a Rapha "Gentlemen's Ride"?

I read on their web site that a Rapha Gentlemen's Ride is "...a ride that involves a little bit of bragging rights but it's more about storytelling and local folklore. It's competition but not to the exclusion of camaraderie and experience. The reality of course is that gentlemen's riding is racing in a group. In fact, gentlemen's riding should really be called what it is — gentlemen's racing. Whatever the distance, whatever the route, a Gentlemen's Ride is anything that isn't a sanctioned race. It's a way, in the middle of your Tuesday afternoon ride, to win a cyclo sportive, a brevet or town limit sign, even your local KOM. At the top of a climb, the group will reorganize, for on a Gentlemen's Ride the group ends as it began, together. But along the way, when the ride is at its most challenging, the headwind at its most unobliging, all bets are off. That's when the order of things remains to be decided. Again and again."

I don't know about you, but whenever I hear the word "gentlemen" I think of sleazy guys getting drunk, eating greasy snacks, and watching a stripper on a pole. When I hear the word "racing" I think of full-on, full-throttle, full-testosterone, full-bore risk taking. Crazy, batshit whacko crazy, nutfuck over-the-top risks that include death and horrific injury for the potential reward of a few dollars, maybe some category upgrade points, bragging rights, and the thrill of performing under intense pressure and fear.

The Rapha blurb confirmed all of this and did so proudly. "All bets are off." "Anything that isn't a sanctioned race."

The most telling quote of all? "That's when the order of things remains to be decided." Ah, of course, it's all about the pecking order, the holy and beloved ranking of dicks.

I've been on zillions of rides like these. They are fuck-the-loser, die-for-the-sprint-sign, last-one's-a-fred, let-Dog-sort-'em-out killfests. The only thing those rides were missing was an entry fee, a waiver, race insurance, enforced safety by licensed officials, field limits, on-hand emergency medical care, and, most importantly, riders roughly sorted by ability and experience.

As crazy as it sounds, certain aspects of these rides typify the best and most appealing side of competitive cycling. They are fun. They are challenging. They test your physical and mental limits. And since the competition is all in your head, everyone's a winner whether your goal is finishing, hanging on, or taking the sprint for the city limit sign. Everybody gets a ribbon, a pecker check, and a rehash at Peet's. Other aspects of the group ride, like organization and safety and help for the weak? Not so much.

So what was Robert Hyndman's last ride really like?

Steve Carre, the co-owner of Bike Effect and organizer of the ride, started a group meet-up specifically to be inclusive. As a boy with four sisters he was always sensitive to women customers who would come in, buy a bike, and leave the shop with that "Now what?" look. So he began a ride that focused on skills. The concepts were that there would be no hammering, no one got dropped, everyone learned how to call out objects in the road, riders practiced basic group etiquette, looked out for each other and didn't go too far beyond their abilities.

On the morning of the ride Steve emphasized that everyone had to obey the rules of the road. The ethos of the ride was that "Gentlemen know when to go hard and when to go easy. You don't need to go off the front and pull crazy hard all the time. Mellow and easy are okay; know when to go."

The group stayed together and was mellow all the way to Topanga. As the riders climbed Topanga, a long and moderately challenging ascent, the group broke up due to the riders' varying ability levels but never went full gas, and the same measured climbing pace happened once they hit Old Topanga. The ride went up Mulholland and Stunt, got stretched out, and regrouped at the top of Stunt. The members of the group were looking out for each other, and at the top of Stunt it was confirmed that everyone knew the route. Some riders chose to go down Fernwood, perhaps because the Las Flores descent was too hairy. Yet the point also has to be made that once you're at Stunt, unless you have a helicopter your choices back down to Pacific Coast Highway are limited to Las Flores, Tuna, Fernwood, or Malibu Canyon. Las Flores and Tuna are terrifying and technical and tough. Fernwood is easier yet highly technical in parts and has more traffic. Malibu Canyon has lots of high speed car traffic and a tunnel.

In any event this ride wasn't a hammerfest, and although there wasn't a detailed description of the descent, Steve provided more support than the average group ride.

Who chose the course?

I learned that Steve chose it, but I learned more than that. According to him, in hindsight it was a poor choice and he holds himself accountable for it. He will carry the guilt of it forever. A stream of friends, of fellow cyclists, and the victim's own brother sought to divest Steve of this responsibility.

"Robert died doing what he loved."

"Shit happens."

"Don't blame yourself. The route wasn't the problem."

"You can't saddle yourself with this awesome burden."

Far from trying to divest Steve from responsibility I applauded him for taking it. By holding himself accountable he showed the mettle of a man and of a leader. By placing the blame on his own shoulders he gave others traumatized by this horrible accident a focal point, and by taking on the burden for himself he lessened the burden of others. He also put to rest, as the man who organized the ride, the suggestion that it was a good course or a suitable one. It wasn't. Why? Because someone died on it. End of analysis.

This of course is what leaders do and it separates them from sheep. People who organize bike rides, who sell and promote the healthful and happy benefits of cycling must, if they are to be people of integrity, acknowledge the other side of cycling as well. It's the side that we have uppermost in our minds when we ride but that we shunt off into a corner of our brain and pray never happens to us. The collisions, the spills, the catastrophic encounters with cars — these things are just as real as the camaraderie, strength, and wellness that come from pushing the pedals. If you cycle you are going to crash. The only question is how badly.

I was impressed and humbled at Steve's leadership. It was his ride, his shop, his course, and these were his buddies. He was going to own it if the ride had ended as planned, and he owned it when it claimed a life. Those who would have cheapened his courage by deflecting the mantle he elected to wear do no favors to him, to those who were grieving, or to the memory of the dead.

What were the mechanics of the accident?

If our scenario is accurate, Robert crashed because he went too fast around a turn and didn't know how to correct without locking up his brakes. You've never locked it up in a turn? Then you haven't spent much time going downhill fast on a bike.

Robert's brother Carl said that Robert had only been cycling for a couple of years. He mentioned that Robert had ridden many roads that were harder and more difficult than Las Flores. Patrick Brady, writer for the Red Kite Prayer cycling blog, said in a column about the accident that Robert had "considerable skill," but in the same breath admitted he didn't know him and had never ridden with him. Patrick is a friend, but I've never heard him praise the skills of a novice cyclist with whom he has never ridden. To the contrary, Patrick is well known for keeping his distance, particularly on descents, from people in whom he doesn't have complete confidence. He's not necessarily a snob, he's just been in too many situations where the less skilled make life dangerous for the skilled. And Patrick is no stranger to the dangers of Las Flores. He had a terrible crash on the descent a little over a year ago.

I'll get to the difficulty of Las Flores later. For the moment let's assume that Robert really was an avid and experienced cyclist with three years under his belt including rides that contained a lot of challenging terrain. Let's also assume that he had considerable skills but with the caveat that there are only so many descending skills that a man in his late forties can pick up in his first three years of cycling.

Descending is a skill that takes years and years of practice to become good at. Many cyclists never become comfortable going downhill even after decades of doing it. At age fifty-one Robert had only been learning to descend for three years at the most. Like so many other skills, the reactions and coordination required to descend are harder to learn the older you get. Even in the best case scenario Robert was a talented novice making a run down a steep and twisty course. In a worst case scenario he was an unskilled novice riding much too fast on a technical and dangerous descent.

According to his brother Carl, Robert was an enthusiastic yet cautious rider. Putting all these anecdotes together, it seemed to me that he was a solid rider but hardly an expert descender. There is one photo I saw of Robert that indicated from the setup of his frame that the chance is quite low that he was an expert or even a very skilled downhiller. This bike was set up with a spaced, high handlebar, and was not optimally set up for a tricky descent. Indeed, it suggested that he may have had back pain or that there was something about the lower, more tucked position of a racing/descending profile that was either uncomfortable, unnatural, or simply unappealing to him. His weight would have been on his rear wheel and his raised shoulders would have further pushed his weight on the back of the machine rather than distributing it evenly along the line from seat to bars.

The even distribution of weight is crucial in tough descents because it allows you to make minute corrections as the road changes simply by slightly moving. When the weight is poorly distributed, corrections require bigger, more radical movements. His center of gravity would have been high as well. The photo and a WAG from one of the people on the ride put him at perhaps six feet tall and about 170 pounds.

Does anybody out there know what happens when a larger guy raises his center of gravity and also shifts his weight onto his back wheel when doing a steep descent? Exactly. He locks the rear wheel when he tries to correct after hitting a turn too hot. This sounds like what happened to Robert and it suggests that he wasn't prepared for the descent even though he looked slim and fit in the photo.

This is hardly a swipe at Robert. Expert descending is almost always the result of a witch's brew of skill and brains and balls and falls and reactions and lots and lots of miles and racing and testing and practicing and training and group rides and comparing notes and pushing envelopes and course memory and tires and ambient humidity and road temperature and frame setup and instinct and the ability to see, just a tiny bit, around blind corners, which is another way of saying "luck."

The chances were good that Robert was out

of his league in the sense that at the time he crashed he didn't know the road, that the bike got going too fast, that he didn't have the skills or experience or setup to bring it back under control, and that his difficulties happened in exactly the wrong place at exactly the wrong time.

How tough is the Las Flores descent?

I had to take issue with the description of Las Flores given by Robert's brother. He said "The terrain wasn't unusual, too risky or unfamiliar. We had ridden this kind of terrain and far harder many times before." Yet we knew this was Robert's first time down Las Flores, therefore it was, by definition, completely unfamiliar. More than simply unfamiliar, for a first-timer, regardless of skill, Las Flores is an alien deathscape laden with traps and tricks. Even the statement that they had ridden "this kind of terrain and far harder many times before" speaks volumes about their skills. Every descent is different, and no skilled descender assumes that a downhill even one road away is similar to the current one.

In my experience there's no such thing as "far harder" than Las Flores. I've ridden in Colorado, in Europe, and throughout the mountains of Japan, and after thirty years of going up and going down on a bike, I've run across a handful of descents as beastly as Las Flores. There are descents that are harder in that they are longer, or they have tighter turns, or they are on narrower roads, or because it's your first time down. But "far harder" than Las Flores? It is a white-knuckled descent no matter how many times you go down it and it demands all your ability every single time. There are no exceptions.

Various people posted or blogged that Las Flores was pretty ordinary for a descent, or that they go down it all the time and it's NBD, or they suggested that there was nothing questionable or unsuitable about this downhill. That's crazy.

My best descent on Las Flores was 29.6 mph, good enough for 11th place on Strava at the time, and I can tell you that even at much slower speeds it is always dicey. The first hard right turn before you drop off into the trees is off camber, incredibly tight, and comes after a series of gentler turns with a short, straight drop that instantly ramps up your speed. It is a shocker and a hard corner to handle every single time.

The twists en route to Hume are treacherous because the road is spiked with debris and because it includes steep ramps, more off camber turns, insufficient room for oncoming traffic, narrow lanes, and speed, speed, speed. When you get to PCH and touch your rims after a Las Flores descent they are so hot they burn your fingers. I've seen good riders who know the descent intimately spill it on this downhill. Larger riders regularly blow out tires from overheated rims.

Patrick Brady's blog described it as "a challenging descent." He also pointed out that the

SETH DAVIDSON

previous Bike Effect group ride descended Tuna, an even harder descent, without incident. Patrick knows every inch of the pavement of every single descent in the Santa Monica Mountains. He has given descending lessons at local bike shops. It took me three years of assiduous practice just to get where I could keep him in sight on descents like Las Flores, and the fact that he recently crashed there and ripped away part of his face is testimony to how hard this downhill can be.

If it was "challenging" for Patrick, that means one thing and one thing only to novices, or first-timers. It is dangerous as hell.

So I don't believe that Robert was in his element. To the contrary, I believe that he was out of it. All of us have been there before and will be there again. It's no disgrace and no dishonor to be sliding sideways on Las Flores Canyon Road. But is that really all it was? Was it just a tough road, an inexperienced rider, and some bad luck?

Risk v. Danger, or bad judgment?

The most cogent apology put forth for what happened was Patrick's, which essentially said that "First, by calling the ride 'too dangerous' we dishonor a skilled cyclist. Second, we denigrate a spectacular land formation and discourage people from enjoying what it has to offer."

The first apology I tried to deal with above. Robert wasn't skilled enough to handle this tricky

256

descent and it is no dishonor to point out that he got in over his head, even though eyewitness accounts have him descending with caution, and even though he was described as a careful guy. The second apology doesn't work, either. No one has suggested that Las Flores be off limits, or that novice riders shouldn't have a go. My suggestion is something different, and not dissimilar to a post found on a site maintained by Speedbloggen. Before we rope new riders into new and challenging terrain on big group rides where they are left to sink or swim, we have an obligation to educate, hand hold, and care for them. Who among us does that? Who among us did that for Robert?

And even if Robert had been warned and had known what he was doing and was just a victim of bad luck, the fact that he's dead means that we need to look at the bigger picture, i.e., what happens when someone new shows up on your ride?

The old ways no longer work

In 1983, when I joined my first group ride, I was the new face, singular. The Freewheeling group rides in Austin on Sunday had a new rider infrequently, maybe a handful in an entire year. Everyone else was a veteran and there was no shortage of advice. I was treated like a newbie but I was also educated. Cycling was a fringe activity and it grew slowly. New faces were easily spotted and dealt with and absorbed. People took the time to tell me what was coming up and what to expect, which was generally an ass beating.

Those days are dead and gone. Most big rides have numerous riders with three years' experience or less. There's no trail boss. There's no cadre of surly, weathered, hardened, experienced bastards who'll shout instructions or pull you over. To the contrary, the old hands either split the field and ride off on their own or they hide from the new crowds. The old guard rides in the wee hours, trading emails among themselves, and they avoid big groups like the plague because so few of the new cyclists know anything about how to safely ride a bike. It's elitist and snobbish, but if you like riding with people whose abilities you know and trust there's little other choice.

Moreover, on their precious Saturdays and Sundays the old school doesn't particularly want to spend its time giving riding lessons. They want to cycle, talk, and enjoy themselves.

With the swell of interest in the sport it's utterly common to see beginners in Los Angeles County with $8,000 rigs. They have the accoutrements of speed but they don't have the intimate knowledge of the route or the skills to match the rig, and there will be thousands and thousands more of them before there are less. We can't expect them to learn by assimilation or by trial-and-error unless we're comfortable with an ongoing roll call of the dead and catastrophically injured.

How we all failed Robert Hyndman

As the Speedbloggen post pointed out, riding is fun but at its core it's serious business. It's serious because the potential for injury and death is great when things go wrong. Even as we try to get more people involved in this thing that consumes so many of our waking hours, we forget that the responsibility for bringing people into the circle is an awesome one. Derek the Destroyer put it this way. "I'd never get my wife into cycling. There's so much that can go wrong, and as a beginner you're aware of less than two percent of the things going on around you that can leave you catastrophically injured or dead." In this sense, Steve Carre is a man among men for being the grown-up in the room and taking responsibility.

In another sense, though, Steve's got no responsibility for what happened, and neither does Robert, his brother Carl, Rapha, or Las Flores Canyon Road. We cyclists have created and encouraged a group ride culture of speed and competition without first doing the basics, which means checking with the new faces, explaining to first-timers the details of the ride, posting information ahead of time so that people know what to expect, and most of all, letting everyone know that it's okay to be the last one down the hill.

We get so caught up in the unsanctioned racing of the group ride that we leave newcomers to figure it out the way we did, by getting shelled, by sliding out in the corner, or by hanging on through Dog's grace and the sheer luck of the dumb. With so many people on the road and so many cars and so many new faces, this approach no longer works. The old hands and the good descenders know that the most dangerous place on a hairy descent is proximity to a poor descender, so we shoot off ahead and leave them to their own devices. Several of my friends who were on Robert's last ride admitted to doing just that.

Each one of us can honor Robert by taking note of the guy or the gal we've not seen before and sharing what we know with them. Whether they're new to the sport or just new to the neighborhood, it's time we did what others did for us back in the day, or should have done, which is to say reach out, share, include. Knowledge in this case isn't power. It's the difference between life and death.

My heart went out to Robert's family, to his friends, to those who were with him on the ride, and to Steve. Nothing will change what happened or really make sense of it, but thanks to Robert Hyndman, maybe we can be better riders, and much more importantly, be better people as well.

YOUR STUPID LIFE

Me: "I'm not very introspective."

Friend: "But you seem to write a lot about your life."

Me: "That's not introspection. It's narcissism."

One afternoon at CotKU

I had stumbled in after a mid-morning ride to get a big black triple-shot of get-me-through-this-fucking-day. The nice girl poured my coffee and I sat down at the giant wooden table they'd recently put in to make the intergalactic franchise look more like an indie coffee shop. I stared at the coffee in the big ceramic mug and remarked at how sad and lonely it looked, topped off as it was with non-fat milk rather than with the gooey, fat-studded chunks of heavy cream that, like pink unicorns, populated my dreams most of the time.

Two pretty women sat down at the far end of the table. One of them was troubled. They glanced at me to make sure I was minding my own business, which made me stare even more listlessly at my coffee and listen with all my might.

The pretty blonde asked her friend, "So what's on your agenda today, Janey?"

The pretty brunette answered, her face

contorted in pain. "The usual stuff. Laundry. Gonna meet this afternoon with the girls from book club. Then fix dinner. Check the kids' homework. Listen to Brian complain about his job. It's all so stupid. God, my life is so stupid, Anne. It's so stupid."

Anne reached across the table and grabbed her friend's hand. "It's not stupid. Why's it stupid?"

Janey didn't say it but a huge wave of my-life-is-passing-me-by swept over the table. "All these things, what's the point? I'm just taking up hours in the day. It's all so pointless. And stupid." She was crying now.

"It's not stupid!" the other woman answered, and she spoke with the warmth and compassion of a true friend. "Think of all the people who love you. Think of all the people for whom you're a ray of happiness and light! Think of your kids who love you and to whom you're the world. That's not stupid! That's as far away from stupid as life gets."

Janey was crying so hard that her shoulders shook.

I gripped my coffee cup tightly, feeling it burn my palms as I tried to keep looking listless. But what I really wanted to do was jump up and give that crying lady a hug and say, "It's not stupid! Listen to your friend. If your life is stupid then all of our lives are stupid. There aren't any stupid lives, only people who don't have someone sitting next to them when they need it most to remind them that it's not stupid, that their lives have meaning and are important even if they don't feel it at that very second. Our lives are not our own!"

My hands were trembling from the pain of the hot coffee and from Janey's pain too, I guess. I'm kind of a pain conductor that way. I was frozen with fear for this nice young lady and her sadness. I wanted to say to her, "My brother thought his life was stupid but after he took it, it just proved how stupid his life really wasn't. We're destined never to see who and how and why we are what we are, but don't mistake that for a stupid life. Please, please, don't."

I was sweating now and took a bored sip of coffee.

The two friends had stopped talking. The lady had stopped crying and the other woman was saying something that made her smile. It was a beautiful smile and as the corners of her mouth turned up, her eyes crinkled. She had the prettiest eyes I'd ever seen. I couldn't hear what they were saying any more; the sounds inside my own head had drowned out everything else.

Suddenly I had to go and couldn't even finish the coffee. I would have hugged her if I'd dared, and thanked her and told her that she'd helped a stranger, a stranger who loved her anyway.

BROKEN RECORD

I hate to be the one to break your Strava bubble, but "PR" is an oxymoron. There's no such thing as a "personal record," any more than there's a "personal Super Bowl victory" or a "personal presidential election."

A record is a mark set by someone that at least two people have done. You know Chris Horner's time up Mt. Palomar? That is a record. Eleven hundred people have done it on Strava and his time is the fastest. It's a record time.

Even though when you climbed it on Tuesday two and a half hours slower than Chris and it was the fastest of your fifty attempts, it's still not a personal record. It's two and a half hours slower than the record. You can call it your personal best. You can call it your fastest time up Mt. Palomar. You can call it proof that your $2,000 power meter and $15,000 bike and $950/month personal coaching regimen are making you faster, but it still pegs you in about one thousandth place relative to the record, and there's nothing personal about it.

All cycling metrics point to one conclusion: You suck

Strava's business model is simple. Provide data to wankers that shows they're getting better.

Since few of us are getting better and all of us are getting older and therefore worse, and since those of us who are improving quickly reach a plateau, there has to be a way to snake-oil us into thinking that we're improving.

So Strava sells us a premium membership where we can compete within a smaller subset of records (age 65+ men with an inseam of less than 25" who sleep on the left side of the bed), and thereby convert some of our meaningless "personal records" into something more meaningful. That something is a higher spot on the age adjusted, inseam-length adjusted, side-of-the-bed adjusted leaderboard.

Unfortunately, even after adjusting ourselves into 75th place, which is a huge jump from 1,000th, physics still mercilessly claws its way to the front. Our "progress" plateaus, and our ability to climb the flailerboard grinds to a halt. So it's back to personal records and chasing the illusion of improvement even though all the data points, or rather, screams deafeningly, to a wholly opposite conclusion. We not only suck, we suck more than we did on this segment last year. Introspective riders feel the icy hand of death tightening its grip around their throat if they look at the data too closely past about age forty.

Note to the Stravati: There's a reason you prefer Strava to bike racing

I don't vomit often but when I do it's usually after someone takes one of my KOM's. I've only got seventeen of them left and there's not a single one that couldn't be handily snapped up by any number of Stravati who live for that kind of thing.

It's no defense but I never tried to set a single one of those KOM's. The handful of times I've gone out and purposely tried to grab a KOM, I've failed. I use Strava for the same reason that I wear pants. It's a social convention the lack of which would earn too much opprobrium. I also use it as a handy calorie counter. And finally, I use it for you. Just when you're starting to think that your performance is dropping off or that you're really not very good, you can click on my most recent ride and feel relief that there's someone in your neighborhood who's slower and an even bigger bicycle kook than you are. This, I believe, is a powerful source of inspiration for flailers and wankers throughout the South Bay. Through Strava I keep them riding. It's a social service and you can thank me via PayPal.

What you can't do is get away with the pleasant little self-deception that your KOM is as good as a bike race. You can't even get away with the delusion that it's as good as an old-fashioned group beatdown on the NPR.

You know why that is? Because it isn't. Masturbating your way to the top of a leaderboard on Strava, when unaccompanied by ball-busting accomplishments on group rides or in real mass start races in which you have to actually pay an entry fee and pin on a number, are just that, digital auto-titillation.

Believe it or don't, I'm fine with that. Riding a bicycle is like consensual sex between adults. I not only approve of it, I'm wholly uninterested in your particular activities. I'm not a libertarian, I'm a "don't give a fucktarian." If you're out pedaling your bicycle, in my book you're winning.

If your riding is confined to setting Strava records without racing or group riding, though, you are wanking. Can we be clear about that? Good. Because last Thursday a new South Bay cycling record was set. It wasn't set on Strava, where anonymous, zipless riders virtually compete using all manner of tricks, traps, aids, pacers, run-ups, and "special assists" to set the record. No, this Thursday record was set the old-fashioned way. Clubbers clubbed. Baby seals got their heads staved in. Pain was ladled out in buckets. And only the strong, the ornery, the mutton-headed, and the relentless survived.

One thing that's never happened on the New Pier Ride

...is a successful four-lap breakaway. Bull and I once, on a cold, rainy, windy winter day in 2012 attacked on Vista del Mar and stayed away for four laps, but it wasn't a real breakaway. We sneaked off three or four miles before the real ride began, there was not much horsepower in the field, and no one even knew we had attacked. Although we hurt like dogs and congratulated ourselves for the heroic effort it was more of a flailaway than a breakaway. Plus, no one cared. To the contrary, they abused us with the worst torture known to the victors in a group ride breakaway. "You were off the front? If I'd known that I'd have chased."

Last week, though, word went out that MMX was coming to town to do the NPR. This meant one thing only, namely that a merciless beatdown was in the offing.

There were at least a hundred baby seals at the Manhattan Beach Pier when the ride left at 6:40 AM. We hit the bottom of Pershing and the peloton immediately strung out into the gutter and then snapped. The Westside baby seals were all lounging on the roadside atop the bump because they've learned from repeated beatdowns that it's better to jump in after the first hard effort than to try and jump in as the group comes by at the bottom of the little hill. Just as they were finishing their first bucket of raw mackerel we came by like a whirlwind.

As we passed the Parkway, Oliver Stanley drilled it, then Cookie drilled it, then Walshy drilled it. MMX, who had started at the back and worked his way up to the point, later noted that from the bottom of Pershing it was pure mayhem. Many of the baby seals were killed with that first single devastating club to the head. Others were so stunned by the acceleration that they simply pulled over, unclipped, and skinned themselves.

Dude with the Funny Helmet reported that this was his 128th time up World Way ramp and it

turned out to be his single highest average wattage
ever for a lap on the NPR, numbers that he churned
out while stuck at the back of the herd after the break
had already left.

After the ramp, G$ blasted away, stringing it
out into a line of about fifteen riders, with a small
clump forming at about sixteenth wheel and turning
into an amorphous lump into which eighty or ninety
baby seals still cowered. After G$ swung over, MMX
opened the throttle, dissolved the clump and
stretched the entire peloton into a single line as
countless little blubbering seals began snapping and
popping like plastic rivets on a space shuttle.

We turned onto the Parkway in full flight with
Walshy, Black Sheep, Oliver Stanley, and "26"
pounding the pedals. This is the point where after the
initial surge the front riders usually slow down, or the
neverpulls in back make their first and only real effort
of the day to chase down the nascent break. Black
Sheep, Walshy, Oliver Stanley, and 26 kept going and
were soon joined by G$, Tri-Dork, Manslaughter,
some dude from La Grange who was incinerated
shortly thereafter, and Haunches, one of the South
Bay's legendary purple card-carrying, neverpulling
wheelsuckers extraordinaire.

MMX looked ahead from the pack as the
break gained ground, then he surged and bridged to
it. When he reached the break he closed the door and
threw away the key. No legit break had ever stayed
away on the NPR for all four laps. The course

generally won't allow it due to stoplights, the high tailwind speeds of the chasing field, and the relatively flat nature of the course.

We made the first turn and had a gap. Atop the bridge Tri-Dork unleashed a monster pull, but then, over his head by the extreme effort, he and G$ were unable to latch onto the break as it accelerated at the next turnaround. Accounts differ, with some claiming a car pinched them, and others claiming they were too gassed to catch, but in any event the break didn't feel like waiting as there were already too many Big Orange kits in the group. This meant the duo of Tri-Dork and G$ had to chase.

The pack was in a different time zone but since we'd only completed one lap there was plenty of time for the peloton to get organized and chase in earnest. What we didn't know is that they were already chasing in earnest, and the stoplight dogs would be smiling on us the entirety of the ride.

Having taken the initiative in trying to fend off the entire baby seal population of the South Bay, we were being rewarded with a string of green lights even as the baby seals were being punished with reds. Naturally, post-ride the baby seals chalked everything up to the traffic signals rather than the sheet-snot that covered our faces and the haggard, beaten look of those who rode the break for the entire four laps.

On the final stretch, after berating Haunches for never coming through, MMX unleashed the leadout. Haunches, suddenly discovering that with the end in sight he wasn't quite so tired after all, leaped just in time for his engine to blow and his legs to detach from his torso. Manslaughter sprunted around the MMX lead-out with Oliver Stanley fixed on his wheel. Going too far out and in too small a gear, Manslaughter settled for second.

We celebrated this, the first ever four-lap breakaway on the NPR, with coffee and sunshine.

And yes, it was a record.

YOUR LIFE IS NOT YOUR OWN

Come meander with me.

But before we join one another on an easy Saturday morning pedal, sharing our love for the road, sharing our camaraderie and our sharp memories of Steve Bowen made sharper by the memorial ride on which we're about to embark, I'd like you to sit for just a moment in the back seat of my car.

It is an old car in dog years, a 2002 Camry with 198,000 hard miles on it. It has a big dent in the rear, a deep rusted scratch on the right side, several beauty marks on the front bumper and rust speckling on the hood. When you sit in the back seat you'll notice several patches of duct tape over the electronic window controls. That's to keep me from reflexively hitting the "down" switch to the driver's side window and having it pop out of the frame and dangle outside the car, on the freeway, at seventy-five.

I want you to sit in the back seat and observe. You'll be invisible. I won't even know you're there.

Hold back the tears

That's the name of a song by Neil Young and you're listening to it with me in the back seat. The song isn't working, because I'm crying and crying hard. It's the first time I've cried for my brother since he died. You're a little embarrassed for me. I'm a grown man, after all.

But you and me, we've ridden together and you know that I may crack but I'm going to recover, pull it together, and keep slogging ahead. I learned that much from Fields. There's no dishonor in getting shelled, only in quitting. Sitting in the dark in the parking garage I check my phone.

"Wow," you think. "Dude is so addicted to Facebook."

But you notice I'm not scrolling through "likes" and timelines. I'm reading, then re-reading, a message from Raja.

"That's weird," you think. "He and Raja have never met."

Indeed we haven't. Then you watch me call Raja, who has messaged me his phone number.

"Hey, brother," you hear Raja say. "Good to hear your voice."

Just like that the two strangers talk like old friends because they are. "How you doing?" Raja asks.

I tell him the truth.

"Well, Seth," you hear Raja say. "Your life is not your own. If your brother had known that maybe he would still be with us. Your life isn't this thing that's yours. That's just a fake construct. Your life is the series of things you say and do to other people, and every vibration of your life touches everyone connected to you and all the people connected to them. We can't take life away casually because it's not ours to take. We have to live if we're to own up to the awesome responsibility we have to those who are bound to us."

You watch me furrow my brow and I listen as intently as I've ever listened to anyone in my life.

"Here's the thing, Seth. I'm an athletic guy in great shape, but you know, a few weeks ago I had a major heart attack. One or two beats away from death, right? I'm one of those cyclists who's not supposed to get sick, let alone have heart problems. But here I am, a heart patient, and you know, everything looks more precious to me now. The people who were there for me in my hour of need, they've touched me just like I've touched them, just like you've touched me, just like I'm touching you. It's the web of life and your poor brother, man, if only he'd known that maybe he wouldn't have taken what wasn't his to take. But you know it now and I know it now. So we will carry on no matter what."

Then you hear me mumble something and you see me put down the phone.

You thought this: "Strangers and near-friends, dear friends and loved ones, people reaching out to people because that's what binds us together, because our lives, however personal, are not our own. They are not our own."

Better start meandering soon

Saturday dawned clear and cold and even before we'd thrown a leg over our bikes Steve Bowen's memorial ride had begun. Susan Gans had gotten the word out to the entire La Grange club. She'd contacted Ellen Brown and Jeff Sallie at Catalina Coffee and arranged for free coffee and tea after the ride. When she told them that they might end up providing free beverages for over a hundred riders they never flinched.

Somewhere along the grapevine Cynergy Cycles in Santa Monica heard about the ride. Without being asked they saddled up their shop van and provided free transportation to westsiders who wanted to come down to the South Bay and join the ride. Then, Jim and Eric from Cynergy used the van for sag and as a broom wagon and escort, running their flashers to keep the cycling cordon intact. Paul Che of Sprocket Cycles was there too, providing support to any rider who needed it.

Cruising down the hill

I've picked you up at Malaga Cove. You're freezing, as it's in the high 30's and you're wrapped up in everything you own, but the clothes still aren't working. We pedal down some more chilly downhill and pick up Marcella on the other side of PCH. You think you're cold? She's chattering so hard she can barely talk.

We hit Catalina just as Gussy, Toronto, New Girl, and a couple of others whiz by in the other direction. We turn around and grab their wheel as they easily tow us up to the bluff above Rat Beach. Marcella is having a hard time just being on her bike. It's the first time she's ridden since Steve's death. She was with him when he died on Mulholland. They had shared thousands and thousands of miles together on the bike. That makes you into more than a friend. That makes you family.

Marcella hadn't wanted to do the memorial ride, intense as it was going to be, and now, with the frigid weather and with her already frozen to the core, you and I can tell that she's in a bad place. Let's put our arm around her shoulder and suggest we head back to the coffee shop in Redondo. I was going to get there early for the ride anyway, and we'll see Gussy & Co. when they circle back for the start.

If three's a crowd, what's three hundred?

We get Marcella some hot coffee and the Cynergy van pulls up. Out hop Cheryl Parrish, Lisa Giardino, Miki Ozawa, Deborah Sullivan, and a couple of others from the Westside. Before long the coffee shop has over fifty people in it. Some are South Bay riders who leave from here every week with the Donut Ride. Many others are from distant locales. Slim has driven up from San Diego and is chatting out front. MMX got in the night before from Carlsbad but a sudden stomach bug has kept him in bed. We're going to miss him. We'll also miss Douggie, one of the South Bay stalwarts. His major knee surgery was recent and he is still on the mend. You can't do a ride like this with a sliced up knee unless you're made out of some stern stuff.

You're looking at me now and I know what you're thinking. "What the hell is going on? There must be two hundred people milling around out there." Indeed there are and it's time to go. We gather everyone together and it's an ocean of people we love.

Our one big fear

You watch me give a brief talk. It's inadequate and bumbling but you and everyone else are gracious and, more importantly, are focused on our memories of Steve. We continue to be deluged with stories of his friendship and goodness, of his decency and humanity, of his acceptance of people for who they are and for how they are.

Marcella is feeling it, too. I've taken her under my wing, or at least under my pink socks. She's starting to see how deeply Steve was loved. Everyone closes their eyes for a moment of silence. Then we roll out.

Michael Norris is there. His presence is comforting. With Michael around, we know that nothing can go wrong, but still we're worried. We're worried because this ride has become so huge. By day's end we'll learn that people stopped counting at over three hundred and fifty riders. With so many cyclists on the narrow Palos Verdes roads, congestion is guaranteed. The worst thing imaginable would be an accident; someone getting hurt while riding on Steve's behalf would be horrific.

We're afraid of the police, too. When they see this rolling peloton of several hundred people they'll have to take action, and we fear the worst. But you and I look at each other and shrug. "What can we do?"

Michael and I sit on the point, Marcella behind us. The goal is simple. Ride slowly, ride safely. Keep in check any idiots who want to turn it into a bike race.

Up against the wall, lycra-clad-mother

As soon as we cross the border from Torrance into PV we see the dreaded police motorcycle. The cop takes one look at us and flips on his flashers. We look at each other. Even Norris won't be able to get us out of this jam. And given the run-ins we've all had with the Palos Verdes police, the ride's going to end before it even starts. The cop has on his "Bub, this is serious face."

The officer nods his head, whips his bike around, and pulls a hundred yards ahead of us. At the first intersection, a squad car dashes up and blocks all turning and cross traffic.

"What the hell?" you and I say to Norris.

He grins. "Looks like Steve just got himself a police escort."

For the entire length of PV Drive the police create a rolling enclosure, blocking off intersections and preventing Saturday traffic from mowing us down. "Who told them?" I ask Michael.

"Steve worked with a lot of the PV cops, lots of those guys ride bikes. He was a liked and respected friend. And the cops take care of their own."

Marcella had been with LAPD for twenty-two years. "It's family," she says. "Family."

Can't keep a tough man down

As we push up from Malaga Cove, a dude in a red Cynergy jersey taps our shoulder. It's Douggie. "Dude!" I say. "Your knee! How are you even out here?"

Doug grins. "There are more important things in life than a knee," he says. "This is one of them."

We crest the first climb and someone else taps our shoulder. It's MMX. "Hey," he says. "Just wanted you to know I made it."

"Dude!" I say. "You were on death's door last night! You were too sick to go get beer, even."

MMX smiles. Then he takes a breath, as if he's rehearsed the whole thing. But you and I know him, and know that he's composing as he talks, the way jazz musicians play. "The greatest truths are the simplest, you know? Steve had a gift of dealing simply with people, yet he himself was very complex. His gift of simplicity was in breaking down things to their essence, of reaching and helping others reach the simple truth in things, in us. In the most meaningful sense he had a way of letting go of all expectations.

His love came with full acceptance, with celebration of your personhood, your love of riding a bike or maybe your fear of getting on a bike, your trepidation and your bravado — he not only accepted who you were, but found enjoyment in you. We're celebrating his life today, simply by riding our bikes and savoring the simple yet memorable."

It came out smoothly, like music, MMX never needing to catch his breath as his legs rolled the big gear over the climb. He drops back. We don't see him again. Sick or well, fit or not, Steve's friends are making the extra mile, then an extra one on top of that. It's the longest yard, indeed.

Dave Jaeger and Harold Martinez roll up to the front. These two guys can put anyone at ease and they shoot the breeze with Norris. I should be more talkative but I'm not. Words aren't coming easily.

Kenny Lam shoots ahead of us with twenty pounds of camera gear. He's not doing the ride, he's shooting it. Greg Leibert has shown up with a helmet cam. He dashes off through Portuguese Bend and sets up on a rock to chronicle the endless stream of friends.

Paul Che wheels up behind us. "Guys," he says. "I stopped at Calle Mayor to help a guy with his bike. When I finished I got on the end of the group and worked my way up to the front. I didn't get to the front until we reached Lunada Bay."

We look back. The end of the line is invisible. The riders go on forever.

The honor climb

We turn onto the Switchbacks where Steve staged so many hillclimbs. Jon Davy shoots ahead, picks a spot, and peels off some video. Miles Irish blocks the oncoming traffic at the entrance with his truck. He'd be riding if he hadn't shattered his scapula and torn his rotator cuff the week before. Instead he runs interference, keeping us safe. We've lost our police escort and the L.A. County Sheriff's Department has taken over the task of keeping a watchful and helpful eye on our progress.

The Switchbacks are the weekly scene of drama and untold suffering, except today, I realize for the first time, that they aren't. Billy Stone said something earlier in the day redolent with truth. Cyclists love to talk about how much they suffer, but it's complete bullshit. Their suffering stops the minute they decide to stop pedaling. Suffering is what happens when no matter how hard you want the pain to stop, it doesn't stop. Cycling is a hobby, an avocation, a pastime. When you choose to hurt, you aren't suffering. You're choosing to hurt.

Death, disease, grinding poverty, mental illness, loss, these things are suffering. As we move through the turns I feel the truth of Billy's observation. We're fortunate to be here. Pedaling our bikes, no matter how hard, is a gift. It may hurt, but it's not suffering.

You and I glance back at Marcella. She's one

of many today who is suffering. She's suffering the loss of a friend and loved one. No matter how easily she pedals, the pain remains.

Michael raises his hand. We're a quarter-mile from the top. The sky is glorious. The sun has turned the ocean into a deep hue of brilliant blue. The curvature of the coast spreads out beneath us, a viewscape so grand that it takes our breath away, and you and I, we think about Steve. This is truly a day for him. The line of riders stretches back all the way down the Switchbacks, and beyond. "Ease up," Michael commands.

Then you and I watch him push Marcella forward. "This is the honor climb, Marcella. Just you. Now go."

He gently pushes her forward. She bites down on the pedals and moves away from us. We see her sides heaving and her shoulders shaking and we know that it's not from pedaling. You and I, we're crying with her. She crests the hill alone, with three hundred and fifty riders in check.

That was for Marcella, that was for Steve, that was for us all.

Catalina Coffee rendezvous

We get back to Redondo Beach and Catalina Coffee. Robert Min is there and a throng of others are, too. Frank has shown up with Irving, Steve's shop dog. Irving is swaddled in love and attention, same as he was in the shop. Steve's girlfriend Vickie and Steve's cousin Scott have flown in from the East Coast to be with us this morning. Susan Gans has arranged to have a large card placed next to the coffee. Countless riders come up and sign the card, many leaving incredibly poignant messages.

We sit at the table with Pablo Maida, who's driven down from the Westside to show solidarity. Like many of the riders, he didn't know Steve but he had friends who knew him and, well, the cycling family is family.

You look at me and we're both thinking about Raja. We say it at the same time. "Your life is not your own." Pablo looks at us in a bemused way then understands without explanation.

You and I speak briefly with Vickie and Scott. "For every one of the people who showed up today there were another hundred who couldn't come because they had other obligations or they were too far away or they didn't find out about it in time. For every one of the people who showed up today there were another thousand who Steve knew and touched but who don't cycle or who don't cycle enough to keep up with the pace or who aren't in good enough health to do the ride. Steve's web of life connected with countless people. This is one tiny strand of his web."

We hug Vickie and give Irving another pat.

Marcella comes up to us. "So glad I came," she says.

We are, too. We're also drained, you and I.

We've been thinking about this since we got the news and we've been mentally preparing for the ride for a long time. Now it's time to go.

We hop on the wheel of Surfer Dan, Dutchie, Toronto, and Pablo as they roll out for a final climb up Via del Monte, which conveniently takes me home.

You drop me off. I wonder what happened to Norris. He'd accompanied us to the coffee shop, then vanished in the way he often does.

I take a nap and check my email. Bing. There's one from Norris. He left so that he could buy a big sack of pastries and drop them off at the PV Police Department.

Michael's life, you know, is not his own. And he knows it. So did Steve, may he rest in peace.

THE RIDE IS INSIDE YOU

You see, the problem is that you want to keep up with people who you can't keep up with. Some people are weaker than others. No matter how hard they try or train, they won't ever be able to keep up with the faster riders when the whip comes down.

You've only been doing this a short time and you've seen dramatic improvements that most people never see. But you make the terrible mistake of comparing yourself to people who are far above your physical ability. This causes you frustration because you want to be as good as they are, which in your mind means "as fast." I could tell you right now that you're much better than most cyclists I've ever met but because you equate good with fast, you can't grasp my meaning or you think I'm flattering you or you think I don't get it.

But it's you, not me, who doesn't get it.

I've been doing this for over thirty years. I learned early on that there are people with whom I can ride on a pleasant pedal but with whom I can never keep up when they turn the cranks in earnest. It's futile to want to do so and ultimately it can poison the real experience of riding a bicycle, which is inside you.

Many people don't want to believe that the ride is inside them. They think it's on the road, or on Strava, or defined by their average speed, or by the number of miles they've logged, or in their race results, or in the unspoken invitation that allows them to hang with the fast crowd. It isn't.

The ride is that thing inside you that you can no longer hold in. When you exercise it you exorcise it, and its release is intensely pleasurable. It leaves you unknotted for a short while, until the need arises to exorcise yet again. Each time you do it you change a little bit, forever.

The physical activity called bicycling can be measured against the performance of others but you cannot express that which is within you through others. You must first understand what is inside you and express it to yourself.

Over the years I've seen many people get into cycling and then get out of it for all kinds of reasons. The main reason is that they were cycling in order to achieve something. Once they achieved it, or once they realized that their goal was unattainable, they moved on to something else. Others cycled because they thought it would provide them with some sort of material gain only to find that it made them much more strapped for cash than they would have been without it. Fancy bikes and aero wheelsets are expensive.

The ones for whom the experience was the emptiest were the ones who did it solely for the competition.

I am the least competitive cyclist you know. When I ride I'm not trying to beat you. If I were I'd never take a pull, or I'd never race crits, or I'd never upgrade until forced. When I ride I'm experiencing something very private that is frequently dependent on the participation of others but never defined by them. Each person plays a role in my internal ride; those who ride faster and drop me, those who ride slower and get dropped, those who vicariously ride with me on Facebook or Wordpress or YouTube, and those who ride next to me sharing a joke and a laugh or an update on the family.

Do you really know yourself?

If you do, you will see the gift and be thankful for it until your most final breath. If you don't, the gift will not look like the thing that it is, but rather like something that's not quite good enough, that needs to be improved upon, or perhaps like something that you can return to the store and exchange or replace for one in a more fashionable color or with better components.

The ride is inside you, but you have to be brave enough to look into that rather dark place poorly lit and to accept what you find there. It's not, perhaps, what you expect. Yet it is the greatest and most wonderful thing of all.

THE DONUT HOLE

It was a nasty, rainy, windy, cold Friday night, and FB was alive with the chatter of quitters, fakers, freeloaders, pretenders, and wishful thinkers, all industriously polishing their rusty collection of excuses until each one shone with the brilliance of a diamond.

"I hate to clean my bike!"

"It's daaaaaangerous!"

"Weather will clear up later...maybe!"

"My periodization schedule calls for an off-day tomorrow."

"I can't miss Junior's indoor kiddie soccer practice!"

"Clarinet recital — Sallie would be devastated if I missed it. They're only young once, you know!"

"Getting ready for the LAVRA series; track workout tomorrow."

I smiled grimly at each lame excuse, each one a thin veneer to cover the cowering, quaking souls that lay beneath. None of this surprised me. We were in Southern California, the birthplace and stoutest bastion of the fair weather cyclist. Unlike the soldiers of the Great Plains, the warriors of the Northeast, or the sunbeaten marauders of the South, the SoCal cyclist needed only a hint of inclement weather to send him scurrying back under the blankets.

Rise and rain

I awoke at 6:30, went into the kitchen, brewed a cup of blackest rat poison and laced it with cream so heavy that the congealed fat created giant buttery blobs floating on the surface. On cold, rainy days like today the lard formed a protective layer inside my arterial walls and prevented the blood from getting cold. I drank deeply from the life-giving elixir.

Next I slathered on a thick layer of Crazy Alchemy embro, cutting it with water to speed the absorption into my skin. Within minutes a small wildfire began running from my ass down to my toes. Tipping my hat to the elements I even donned knee warmers. After a quick bowl of oatmeal I was off.

The drop down Via del Monte was wet, windy, treacherous, and cold. Unable to pedal much due to the buffeting winds, by the time I reached the Donut launching pad at 8:00 the turnout was just as I had expected. It consisted of the hardest of the hard, the toughest of the tough, the dumbest of the dumb, the flailingest of the flail. I stared stonily, turned my bike around and rolled out.

Let the pain rain down on me

I kept the pace stiff all the way to Malaga Cove, through the stop sign, down the short drop, and then went full throttle. The agony I inflicted was so massive and so sudden that I could imagine the happy smiles of those who had stayed home in bed to quaff Earl Grey tea and lick their strumpets. Would they rather be at home — surrounded by wet strumpets, or here — surrounded by a freezing rain and a wall of pain?

No one came to the front. The Big Orange softmen? Not today. The Ironfly serious cyclists? Nix. The strongmen of team SPY? Nowhere to be seen. Today's strategy was obviously to let Wankmeister pull 'til he blew, flailed, and got dropped.

"Heh, heh," I laughed at the futility of their plan.

Through Paseo del Mar and up the Lunada Bay Elementary bump I kept the gas on, imagining the whimpering, crying, pleading, and begging that might have been going on behind. But today there would be no mercy.

Some days you just have it

I stayed on the front through Golden Cove, battling the wind full gas, and without breaking my cadence I cruised easily through the intermediate sprint. No Prez came shooting by; no one wanted to challenge anything this day. It was written thus in the stars.

By the time I hit the short incline at Trump National Golf Course my legs felt a bit heavy. The cold rainwater had soaked down to my skin, my feet had become chilled and a constant drizzle of rain ran down the inside of my jacket, down the collar of my jersey, through my undershirt and against my back, but never mind. Pain is in the eye of the beholder. However miserable I felt, it would have been worse for anyone behind me. As it had been from Malaga Cove, there wasn't a single rider besides me who wanted to tangle with fate by driving it at the front.

At the bottom of the Switchbacks I jumped hard. I knew no one would come around or even think about coming around. I pedaled on, going harder and faster until the only turning wheels and the only hard breathing I could hear were my own. As I rounded the last turn I glanced back. No one in sight. I cruised up to the college and raised my hands to celebrate this unparalleled victory on the Donut Ride. It was the first time in seven years that I'd soloed to the finish.

I took a moment to savor the feeling of being the strongest, the fastest, and the unquestioned best.

Because that's what happens, you know, when you're the only one who shows.

Made in the USA
Charleston, SC
25 November 2013